The Daily Telegraph

Cryptic Crossword Book
56

The Daily Telegraph

Cryptic Crossword Book
56

Pan Books
in association with *The Daily Telegraph*

First published in 2006 by Pan Books
This edition first published 2018 by Pan Books
an imprint of Pan Macmillan, a division of Macmillan Publishers Limited
Pan Macmillan, 20 New Wharf Road, London N1 9RR
Basingstoke and Oxford
Associated companies throughout the world
www.panmacmillan.com

In association with *The Daily Telegraph*

ISBN 978-1-5098-9374-4

Copyright © Telegraph Group Limited 2006

9 8 7

A CIP catalogue record for this book is available from the
British Library.

Visit **www.panmacmillan.com** to read more about all our books
and to buy them. You will also find features, author interviews and
news of any author events, and you can sign up for e-newsletters
so that you're always first to hear about our new releases.

ACROSS

1 One is not bound to enjoy this (7)
5 Coach, working on American lines (4-3)
9 A unit set to rise and advance is at an advantage (3,2,2)
10 Meantime, if one leaves, it's during school time (7)
11 Bargain to get across (9)
12 Wild party with many a man of music (5)
13 They're often seen in Assisi! (5)
15 Caught sight of rescinded order (9)
17 Paper said to come out and leave no trace (9)
19 Run out of pictures to back (5)
22 Shots of Surrey opener stir the Oval (5)
23 He teaches the student body (9)
25 Lands in Eastern America (7)
26 He makes one cross at times (7)
27 Merit of French verse translation (7)
28 Had the best part marked with an asterisk (7)

DOWN

1 Disposition of uncle to have a fling (7)
2 Comes out East and joins up (7)
3 Station where Dorothy holds the record (5)
4 Knock around with a chap with a title (9)
5 German currency between banks? (5)
6 Come between people (9)
7 Moving home (7)
8 Unkempt politician ruled out (7)
14 Stay to drink and drink (9)
16 Ships carrying the right pennants (9)
17 Finish after only half the distance and stretch out (7)
18 Shows rank subservience (7)
20 A tortuous swindler (7)

21 Revised tale with a colourful ending (7)
23 Article on Man, perhaps, that divides the church (5)
24 Half the operations performed in the theatre (5)

ACROSS

1 Beer perhaps taken to admiral in hold (4,6)
6 Bobby found ring in cage (4)
9 Walk it? It's allowable (5)
10 Interval for the cameraman (4-5)
12 Doll perhaps having a notion but not be serious about putting it into practice (3,4,2,4)
14 Brought up malformed runt with rude disposition (8)
15 Is coming back to obtain new insertion for ring (6)
17 Instruction in naturism? (6)
19 Older members have a party at a fabulous place (8)
21 Surprising intelligence (9,4)
24 Fellow with a brown cap in New York? (9)
25 It's growing inside circular chamber (5)
26 Never coming from North Ayr resort (4)
27 Growing source of electricity? (5-5)

DOWN

1 Tiller and male student with Frenchman (4)
2 Match substitutes craft (7)
3 It doesn't appeal to me at four o'clock (3,2,3,2,3)
4 Left one dry and frozen on this network (8)
5 Go round twice at speed (5)
7 Person living in a town Pop and I upset (7)
8 Prudence following Penny respecting safeguard (10)
11 What a pet cat might do – achieve without effort (4,2,4,3)
13 Native in his castle? (10)
16 Polish eastern angel clumsily on church (8)
18 Composer who has made his mark? (7)
20 Country Stuart shortly revolutionised in song (7)

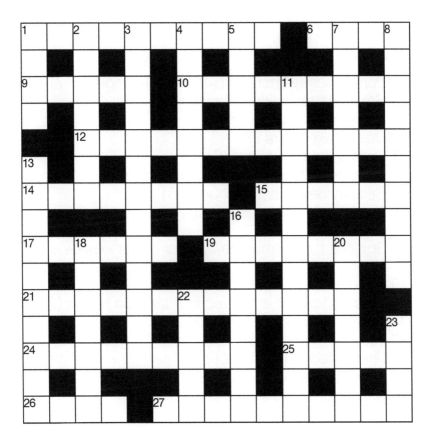

22 Opening passage, anthem stopped short of it (5)
23 Many a hit or a miss? (4)

ACROSS

1 Person set against work – a difficult problem! (7)
5 Small matters slide at break (7)
9 A statement, article, or letter (7)
10 Deal in used cars (7)
11 Gallant old entertainer (9)
12 Nobody will receive can-opener as present (5)
13 Security device left at church (5)
15 Speed with which the managers aim to score here (9)
17 Suggest the German newspaper leader was devious (9)
19 Three – wrong number! (5)
22 A woman carrier employed in Burlington House (5)
23 Front men making a charge (9)
25 Included in general anxiety about the medico (7)
26 Unequalled team's beef (7)
27 Hopelessness assailing the pilgrim (7)
28 Note evidence of leaves (7)

DOWN

1 Gemstone displayed without a twitch of an eye (7)
2 A gratuity for just being there (7)
3 This country is nonchalant – up to a point (5)
4 Marine possibly turning colour due to excess (9)
5 Individual making much of a period with royalty (5)
6 The board accepting a fall may be enlightened (9)
7 Young child standing over a princess (7)
8 Follow progress (7)
14 New fitting ready, hang a decorative plant (9)
16 Memorable revolutionary character (3-6)
17 A fabulous creature, though without standing (7)
18 Loving a large number, love turned sour (7)
20 Listing what may be done at last (7)

21 Set right with regard to the outfit (7)
23 Music maker creating a stir (5)
24 One knows them to be well-informed (5)

ACROSS

8 Short-lived insects may fly close together (8)
9 Only stove in a Dutch house (6)
10 Picking up the idea of the game? (3)
11 Books of *Macbeth* and *Othello*, for example (8)
12 Involving two of brainy disposition (6)
13 Recklessly, I hang about for an English author (7,8)
15 Eccentric, if loud, capital (7)
18 Appropriate, his function? (7)
21 Originally, a quartet in which one player remained tacit (3,4,8)
24 Clergyman takes chlorine little by little (6)
25 Chivalrous chaps irritate workers (8)
26 Collection of sayings in an anthology (3)
27 Spheres of interest in respect of charity (6)
28 Disturbance in which, at home, detectives throw net out (8)

DOWN

1 Arrogant at university? Nonsense! (6)
2 Person presenting Bill Porter (6)
3 Outlook for the software race, in new presentation (7,8)
4 Cut in earnings makes one terribly frightened (7)
5 Means of securing motor-cycle and sidecar (11,4)
6 White powder easing Ma's trouble? (8)
7 Uncontrollable rage could give distress (8)
14 Port always right in Scotland (3)
16 Greek hero sick, with pains all round (8)
17 In modest way, showing object on cathedral (8)
19 Be prone to equivocate (3)
20 A large beer called for a lady's maid (7)

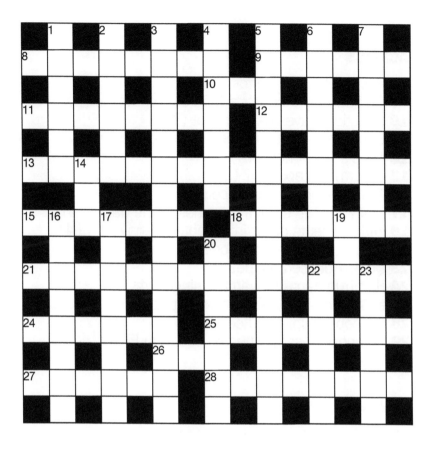

22 Puts away masses we hear (6)
23 Tar assessment (6)

5

ACROSS

1 Points which make for a dilemma (5)
4 So heavenly a herb – a trifle sweet, maybe (8)
10 Sanction leaves us in a spot (7)
11 Sebastian's sister is open to endless abuse (7)
12 Mine's full of holes (4)
13 A worthless apology? (5)
14 The girl's prison sentence (4)
17 Morning star 'e will trail shines in the dark (14)
19 Infringements of art in accepted behaviour (14)
22 Taking tome out, find speck of dust (4)
23 Quaker dessert recipe? (5)
24 Half true name of wartime singer (4)
27 & 30 I've simply no idea what to put here! (1,6,1,4)
28 For pop group, it's sheer bliss (7)
29 Composes essay, unusual satire on ET (8)
30 See 27

DOWN

1 The line for a horticulturalist to take (8)
2 A dish to stir – nothing to it! (7)
3 Locate a bridge in mass panic (4)
5 Stay on ship in Barrie's fantasy world (5,5,4)
6 Take Latin and get on at school (4)
7 Ian's twice taken right nationality (7)
8 So bit it an old penny to change (5)
9 Oddly, police on trains in charge of children (2,4,8)
15 Pinpoint localities (5)
16 A charming accent (5)
18 Ad about get-away to an adventure (8)
20 A violation going without changing gear (7)
21 The total garment (7)
22 How's the weather? I can see nothing in the mist (5)

25 Politician's chair (4)

26 Alcoholics about, about the neighbourhood (4)

ACROSS

1 Not married – is that a record? (6)
5 Found a route one's abandoned (8)
9 The spooky is ordinary to airborne soldier (10)
10 Drawer for cash from work (4)
11 Endlessly hot – no outstanding thing in Hawaii resort (8)
12 Disconcerted by cast (6)
13 Boast of clothes brought back (4)
15 Walking on treacherous gradient (8)
18 Father out more? That doesn't hurt (8)
19 Cry for small coin (4)
21 This will stop you taking a long look (6)
23 Leads are soft – poor working (8)
25 Singer beginning to bray – a donkey! (4)
26 Unwell, unable to shuffle further? (3,2,5)
27 Look again, but it's an academic exercise (8)
28 Pageant is shabby stuff, as well (6)

DOWN

2 Part of America where I had a house briefly (5)
3 Gorgeous instrument in South Wales (9)
4 Passage taken out of book (6)
5 Appear to cancel, but give satisfaction (4,2,2,7)
6 Initially secure place to speak, but rant incoherently (8)
7 Flower festival has no leader (5)
8 Everyone has debts, receiving a state income (9)
14 Money earned off the peg (5-4)
16 Forgo party outside (2,7)
17 Assail with call to switch from Tories? (8)
20 Actor/manager's advice to eat fast? (6)

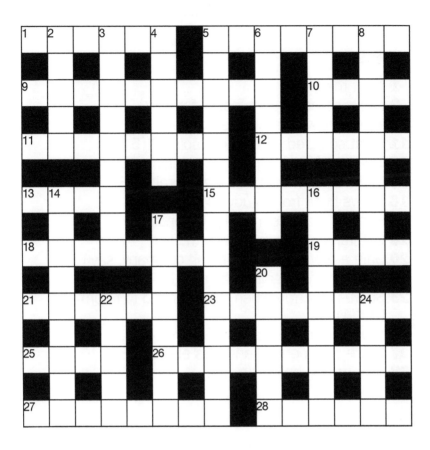

22 Taking a step wrong, use stick (5)
24 Some dissipation on the terrace (5)

ACROSS

1 Neat theft (8)
9 Easily defeat though not in form (8)
10 Thought I would take half of each (4)
11 Spirit conjured up by other spirits? (5,7)
13 Taken aback, finding acid in vehicle (8)
15 Made a mistake that's irrecoverable (6)
16 Draws back from study (4)
17 Ron, for example, may be beyond help (5)
18 Outstanding poem we hear recited (4)
20 Gain a profit from a shipping company, say (6)
21 Checks votes again in details (8)
23 Spares no effort when bosses need to reform (4,4,4)
26 I have a turn on stage in *Othello* (4)
27 Made a comeback and was elected (8)
28 He's having an off-day (8)

DOWN

2 Do we turn switch to produce current? Yes (8)
3 Business figures show what happens after a slump (5,7)
4 Latins put out or put in office (6)
5 He was barbaric in treating others (4)
6 Vagrant who doesn't enjoy walking fast? (8)
7 Strike supported by a devout Buddhist (4)
8 Rose, as the century drew to a close (8)
12 Generating copy (12)
14 One eating in American cafe (5)
16 Criterion followed by a cavalry regiment (8)
17 Fag-end got bent in picking up the pieces (8)
19 Tie up damaged net and fish (8)
22 Thank you, and goodbye! (6)

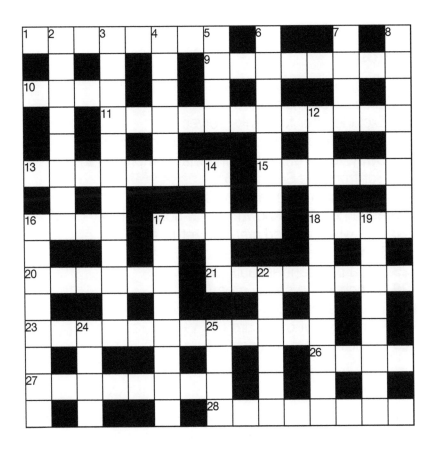

24 Amphibians with feet going in two directions (4)
25 Chemical gives rise to sad behaviour about nothing (4)

ACROSS

1 Ambitious person in the jet-set? (4-5)
9 Excessively musical (6)
10 Exclude offer for drinks server (9)
11 Threaten to come to a devilish conclusion (6)
12 Sway, leave office with internal complaint (9)
13 Hot from the Solent? (6)
17 Used one's teeth a little (3)
19 Become widely known how to obtain money (7,8)
20 Flap when winged creature returns (3)
21 Stick by a detached area of Scotland (6)
25 Not a pleasant assault (9)
26 Blanch left in sandy area (6)
27 Take a short route to slice in two (3,6)
28 Pointedly put on record (6)
29 Politician from America? (9)

DOWN

2 To some extent at home then not at home (2,1,3)
3 Two items of clothing in diminutive lady's make-up (6)
4 Solitary individual getting in £2 on last day (6)
5 Potentially shocking interruption in current (10,5)
6 Before being fully-fledged is too soon (9)
7 He appeals to Ella in a very quiet, novel testament (9)
8 Valuable feature of a lacewing fly (6-3)
14 Was it another strip round narrow part of a garment? (9)
15 Old-fashioned supporter on the field (6-3)
16 I'd come up with two fellows before one sect needing much skill (9)
17 Live with time to gamble (3)
18 Vessel however capsized (3)

22 Inclined to include quintet from the Eastern Mediterranean region (6)
23 In the chaos I risked including an Egyptian deity (6)
24 A match for some holy scriptures (6)

ACROSS

7 Up it goes for viewers in the main (9)
8 Being trendy, acquired a pig (5)
10 Working out latitude and height (8)
11 Involved in one-sided rows, eventually nod (6)
12 Old Peruvian taking a single can maybe (4)
13 A letter with cutting amusing comeback (8)
15 After the game hundreds made complaint (7)
17 Part-exchange can include novel read (5-2)
20 Puts up with relatives – should be on guard (8)
22 Fight for breath, as admitted by the doctor (4)
25 Porridge is a fine alternative! (6)
26 Railway worker in a Manx resort (4,4)
27 Start to cast (5)
28 To inform about top people is squealing (9)

DOWN

1 A writer having fine point (5)
2 Servant wearing a very short skirt (6)
3 Spot-on article about a minister (8)
4 A rider accepting toll has some attraction (7)
5 Raised by a sovereign? (8)
6 Urge to put studies before exercise (9)
9 A hideaway in the Near East (4)
14 Unpolluted space for players' use (9)
16 Mounting a revolt (8)
18 Watched a dredger in operation (8)
19 Check a crawler without cash (7)
21 Understanding the German issue (4)
23 May set out to appear sultry (6)

24 If reflective and close he's a real trial (5)

10

ACROSS

1 Law rests with male hospital attendants (9)
8 Head fuzz? (5,2,6)
11 Second note is a tiny speck (4)
12 Inner pyramid ascertained as resting-place of this king (5)
13 Expedition in direction of ancient city (4)
16 What activity traps family in foul air? (7)
17 Refuse the job of Eliza's father (7)
18 Horatio's ways of seizing opponents (7)
20 Caught in light shoe? It's a disgrace! (7)
21 City street at the end (4)
22 Infant left in the tower, here (5)
23 Amaze with endless acrobatic feat in film (4)
26 Our helicopter adapted for Belgian detective (7,6)
27 The comma in lepidopterist's collection? (9)

DOWN

2 Stalk blown in the wind (4)
3 Some wearing down, for example, around sculptor (7)
4 Boy holding scheme for the country (7)
5 Slippery characters sleep around, mostly (4)
6 Its twin-speakers shatter goblet, unfortunately (6,7)
7 Housing assistance (13)
9 A body of musicians, one at a time, in diverting manner (9)
10 Most advanced military units of top rank (5,4)
14 Epitaph over Yorkshire cathedral (5)
15 Scottish island is non-clerical (5)
19 Sinful, having rook taken by moving castle (7)
20 Earring – one that may drop off (7)
24 Colour from the initial early *cru* (4)

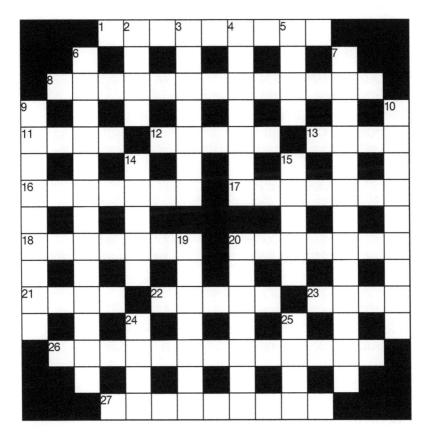

25 Give advance notice of programme (4)

ACROSS

1 Quarter size, but it's out of this world, (6,9)
9 Red China started border issue (7)
10 Respond to alternative power source (7)
11 Polite second-half share statement – again (9)
12 Letter from abroad is returned by Gemma, oddly (5)
13 First school to take care of lines (7)
15 Broadcast at a dire performance (7)
17 Go on about quiet children's toy (7)
19 Raging stream coming from mountain fissure (7)
21 Outstanding sources of original work in native gold (5)
23 Foreshadow a silly price (9)
25 Withdraw passage (7)
26 Stubborn worker chasing original partner (7)
27 Support youth when getting on a bit (6,9)

DOWN

1 Group's loud behaviour (7)
2 Marry, single and free at last (5)
3 Will men at work follow the match? (9)
4 Partners in God's mass (7)
5 Remain confused by source of rock salt (7)
6 Approaches auditor in case of news (5)
7 Don't start retreating in chaos – mingle! (9)
8 Recount how tear ran out (7)
14 True to life, turns tail and cries out (9)
16 Go quickly over directors' target (9)
17 Suit commander to be in the papers (7)
18 Stretching point – in charge after final (7)
19 A must in freak sea conditions (7)
20 Stood round and talked business (7)
22 Smile about a bit of corn (5)
24 A city doctor's fierce encounter (5)

ACROSS

1 Veteran promoter of causes (10)
6 Fool envelops monarch with requests (4)
10 Start rolling stone (5)
11 Faulty clue one takes time to clarify (9)
12 Kind of money in bond (7)
13 Where horses should do their level best? (3,4)
14 Action needed when the ball's landed in your court (6,6)
18 Be dangerously frivolous and light? (4,4,4)
21 Players were ahead, so moved defensively (7)
23 Course included one new procedure (7)
24 Hides note, tampered with illicitly (2,3,4)
25 Pair taking fish to group of cats (5)
26 Awkward twist caused death (4)
27 Highly amused at being sewn up? (2,8)

DOWN

1 Alternative of better quality (6)
2 Get the better of boat captain (6)
3 Airy way to take a short cut? (2,3,4,5)
4 With wild rage, goad elderly relative (5-4)
5 In anger, uptight, is going to explode (5)
7 In stable, I got on horse (8)
8 Pleasant exercise, collecting a fragrant flower (5,3)
9 Impure to kill it, perhaps? There's no choice (4,2,2,4,2)
15 Notes turmoil of postponement (9)
16 False description of credit notes (8)
17 Test case involved plastic box (8)
19 Trout, say, caught in the end (6)
20 Fathers, for example, put in wagers (6)
22 Condescend to hear *Hamlet* (5)

ACROSS

1 The academic field (6)
4 I'm engaged in property valuation (8)
9 It's not often there's real trouble in the railway (6)
10 War that's breaking out in Panama? (5-3)
12 I return to a trivial item (4)
13 Split the pot (5)
14 Born at the *King's Head* – a low joint (4)
17 You'11 be lucky to win one (4,2,6)
20 One whose pupils are encouraged to make notes (5-7)
23 Tree, one found by the river (4)
24 I pick up key to look round Inuit house (5)
25 Forest's administrative fellow (4)
28 It's heard after the raid that nobody is found guilty (3,5)
29 Not how Anne Boleyn's ghost will collide with you (4-2)
30 Pass on the takings (8)
31 Game couple (6)

DOWN

1 Gun-support bearing (8)
2 French husband has a period by the sea (8)
3 This description is hardly fair comment (4)
5 The pleasure of compensation (12)
6 Rain is unusual in this country (4)
7 About to happen soon in the vicinity (2,4)
8 One of two that is set up to the right (6)
11 As set by one out to break a record? (8,4)
15 Humphrey's artless look to us appears phoney (5)
16 Possibly Indian form of canoe (5)
18 The adder is squirming when strung up (8)
19 I forsake the Law for the Artillery (8)

21 One who's learned to park a vehicle in the street (6)
22 PC Skinner (6)
26 Singer has altered a lot (4)
27 Twisted wire could be a danger to riverboats (4)

ACROSS

1 Near to the truth just outside one's front door perhaps (5,2,4)

10 Acted in an unspeakable way (5)

11 Artist chancellor found behind French backwater (9)

12 Informed its possessor (9)

13 No sound from the horse? (5)

14 Modern flood precaution in Nottinghamshire (6)

16 Unrivalled lady took apprentice in (8)

18 Endlessly prejudiced about disease (8)

20 Out in the garden perhaps (6)

23 Seafood press chief disguised (5)

24 Corresponding with a musical sound heard by a group of conservationists (9)

26 Nine trees replanted by a lady (9)

27 Cloak, umbrella etc covered the tarred rope (5)

28 Voice of one's fiancée heard on the telephone? (7,4)

DOWN

2 Arm our leader taking a few steps under the bar (5)

3 Putting something on a horse, he's no better (7)

4 Artist interrupts flow of long sermon (6)

5 Had missing article about current unit that hindered (8)

6 One taken in by Silas, a seaman (7)

7 Blazer that has been put out? (7,6)

8 Is this principal character against taking the lady's ring (8)

9 Contemporaneous nevertheless (2,3,4,4)

15 Inflicting injury that's hurting another's feelings (8)

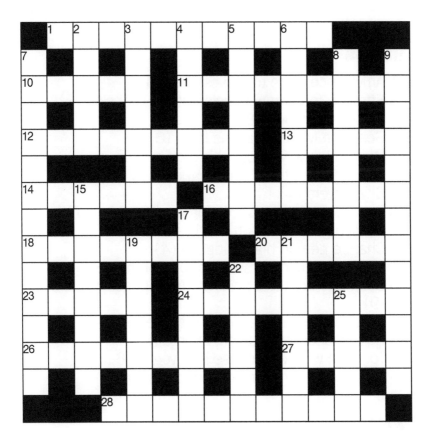

17 After science, one has a twitch, a bout a neuralgia (8)
19 Carroll, Director General getting into another snood! (7)
21 Run round during the fight but become ineffective (4,3)
22 Plan might seem different going round church (6)
25 Invite one to take cover (3,2)

ACROSS

1 Arrive once more to harvest fruit (8)
5 Effective temporary housing at the river-side (6)
9 Knitwear for town (8)
10 Seat unruly sailors at the back (6)
12 Deadlock involving old ship's officer (9)
13 Decoration of the church in the French way (5)
14 Shy players (4)
16 Put out yet again concerning one's petition (7)
19 Medico getting work through a dispenser (7)
21 Change gear in high dudgeon (4)
24 A person who never wanted to leave home (5)
25 Seems to accept a point made by peace-makers (9)
27 Used to coat drunken men with ale (6)
28 Quite reasonable custom charge (8)
29 To judge without purpose is in vogue (6)
30 He'd a date – new tie called for! (4,4)

DOWN

1 Engineers on this French vessel get a break (6)
2 Rating a motorway overseas (6)
3 It's self-respect makes coppers go on (5)
4 Unrelenting six-footer pursuing a mother (7)
6 Viewing outside broadcast and waiting for follow-up (9)
7 Work out tax to accommodate royalty (8)
8 Offered to look after injured deer (8)
11 A beast gaining support (4)
15 Anxiously anticipate arrest (9)
17 A fan – ardent he may well be! (8)
18 Propose no talking bird, note (8)
20 Some people are always genuine (4)
21 Admonish salesman over range available (7)

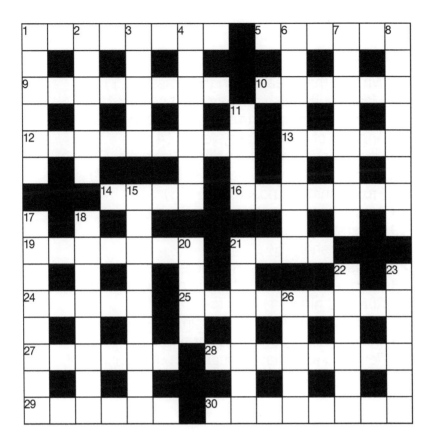

22 Watch out for a worker encompassing conflict (6)
23 Accede as directed (6)
26 Am at the finish, for a change (5)

ACROSS

1 What is that creature on the grass? (11)
9 Mostly outlandish old gambling game (4)
10 Turn him crabwise, trusting to fortune (11)
11 Anguish of one In galley-vessel (4)
14 Lavish, fast time after work at university (7)
16 King of Britain carrying the kid, possibly (7)
17 Project through poetic Wales (5)
18 Activity of those putting back lash (4)
19 Understudy's part in *Animal Farm*? (4)
20 Steal in shop (5)
22 Foolishly ignored signs of deterioration (7)
23 Bond returns unwell, there is no going back (7)
24 Run and hide! (4)
28 Angle head in such canvassing (7,4)
29 Frolic in long-boat of ancient times (4)
30 Resent a kiss that is rough with unevenness of quality (11)

DOWN

2 Once a fine Norse navigator (4)
3 Indicate time in buffet (4)
4 Brian in TV production? Electrifying! (7)
5 Precious few (4)
6 How to remove cap of a French prison-officer? (7)
7 This jumper rides up (11)
8 County ranking can be humbling (11)
12 Granny Smith, for example, on a stick (6-5)
13 Are our dolls falling for Continental bucks? (11)
15 Article of diminished note (5)
16 En bloc, alcoholics accept any pub that is handy (5)
20 Cut favourite piece (7)
21 One's family, mostly benevolent people (7)
25 Attached to church in the old days (4)

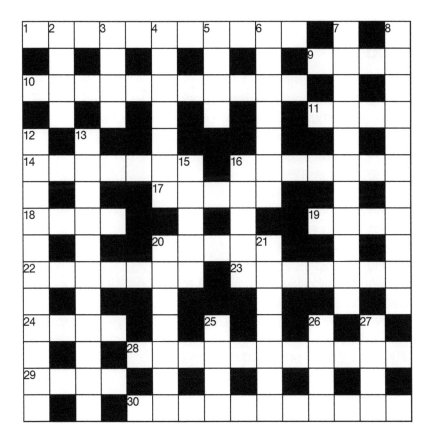

26 Short drive from slow bowling (4)
27 Mixed greens turned endlessly, unfortunately (4)

ACROSS

1 Bearing fish and fruit (8)
5 Used the needle, being on edge (6)
9 Greek article followed by one other article (8)
10 Refits quite possibly causing contention (6)
12 "Act a part?" a certain party scoffed (9)
13 Records some music (5)
14 Face set-back (4)
16 Allowing nothing to restrict the view (7)
19 An Italian engineer's tale (7)
21 The staff will see dawn break (4)
24 Guide always at a holy man's side (5)
25 Warder who likes his intake to be neat? (9)
27 Drops sound rules made (6)
28 Nag when messed about in the country – get really foul (8)
29 Avoid giving points to champ (6)
30 Housing English people in temporary accommodation (8)

DOWN

1 Tart notice about game (6)
2 Puff at this point, but hold on (6)
3 Wild dog in dog compound (5)
4 Ring about ugly old woman wanted by an artist (7)
6 No longer stress the spread (9)
7 Declare support (8)
8 Getting ready and lining up (8)
11 Money? Some hopes of that! (4)
15 One caring inordinately for greenness (9)
17 Keep quiet over book taken (8)
18 He can't remember a figure involved in case (8)
20 Uprising effective in the Mediterranean (4)
21 Come to grips with the opposition (7)

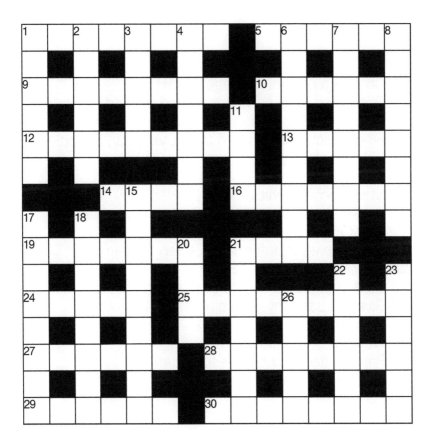

22 A kid totally untroubled (2,4)
23 Many put inside aren't spirited (6)
26 A bore before receiving silver (5)

ACROSS

1 Condition of Abel's dotage? (6,9)
9 One has a local name for wicked sinning (3,4)
10 Back off being in feature – it's thin material (7)
11 From which Britons used to die, we hear, in battle (4)
12 Bird is to cower (5)
13 Mark second vehicle (4)
16 Workers' organisation look over unknown part of Italy (7)
17 Non-proprietary information given to man (7)
18 Dismiss assembly (4,3)
21 Contemptible person, to hire out present (7)
23 Give me back my prize statuette (4)
24 Opera singer's new bed (5)
25 Weakness of deputy (4)
28 Popular dance becomes forgotten (2,5)
29 This painter was all Greek to the Spanish (2,5)
30 Court's wrong view of what may have caused accident? (5,2,8)

DOWN

1 Follow fashion to make current easy progress (4,4,3,4)
2 Seek votes from the cloth, say (7)
3 Unsophisticated note article provided (4)
4 Five scores making landmark for batsman (7)
5 Superficially irritated, but very keen (7)
6 Solution slowly taken in, if you're patient? (4)
7 Policeman to find if force is corrupt (7)
8 Follow the custom – no tipping on board (4,4,3,4)
14 Large house in ruin – no entry (5)
15 Take cocaine, and a swift drink (5)
19 Walker rose (7)

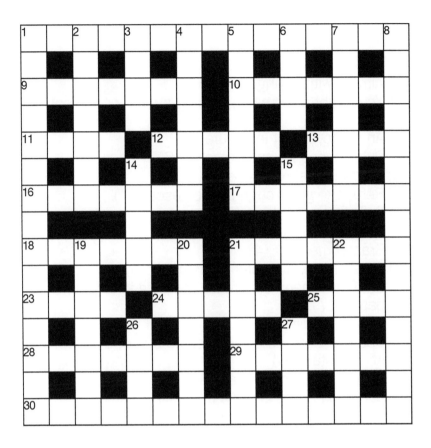

20 Decline to describe Manx cat briefly? (4,3)
21 Dislike a copper coming round vineyard (7)
22 Look hurt, perhaps, if one has this? (4,3)
26 Chieftain Semiramis captured (4)
27 Eagerly expecting silver to go up (4)

19

ACROSS

1 Almost within range? (4,6)
9 You might say it when offering a gift – or present (4)
10 An improvement in culture (10)
11 Publications for entertainers? (6)
12 On board get rotten seats (7)
15 Refuse to go through all the cases? (7)
16 Pulls back the grass (5)
17 Has a tumble in the snow (4)
18 Branch member (4)
19 Great figure, a master to his mate (5)
21 Salad greenery and French dressing in a light basket (7)
22 Infantile habits (7)
24 One must back the law to some degree in this African state (6)
27 Mere agents might make them (10)
28 Such pomposity is not a front (4)
29 In which the reserves run out (6,4)

DOWN

2 It's always right to follow the first mate (4)
3 Was abusive, yet guarded? (6)
4 Irritates by the unnecessary loss of a point (7)
5 Takes advantage and gains three points on centre court (4)
6 At heart he'd a desire to get married (7)
7 From vice I'd reformed in stir, possibly? On the contrary (10)
8 Meals and beers set out for get together again (10)
12 It's wet and fine at the same time (6,4)
13 She serves the school (6,4)

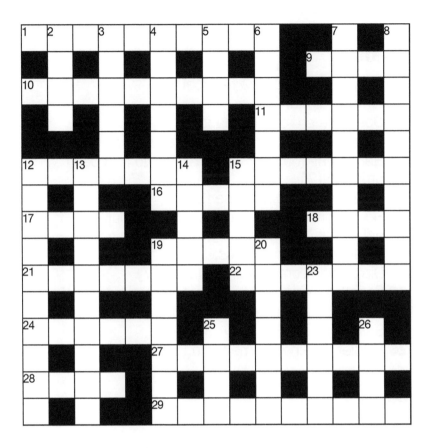

14 Go into liquidation when working hard? (5)
15 New or old slaver (5)
19 Servants turning in between lunch and dinner? (7)
20 Coward and criminal come up in a sailing vessel (7)
23 Expect disturbance in bar (6)
25 He's American at heart (4)
26 It's hotly tipped so raise the stake (4)

ACROSS

1 Lady unaffected by a reversal (5)
4 Always faithful (8)
8 Does one go round firing it? (8)
9 Remarkably happy in eastern festival (8)
11 Had sitting room for about 500 who had been drugged (7)
13 Going from bad to worse (9)
15 How inferior manufacturers added to our difficulties? (4,6,5)
18 Modern country state (3,6)
21 Diplomatic contact fully included (7)
22 Beastly time in the lowest accommodation? (8)
24 Penny saying further, about 50 are using oars (8)
25 Sailors' acid? (8)
26 Soldier obtained some lamb (5)

DOWN

1 Notes lady who is on target? (10)
2 Number getting in split payment (8)
3 Combative left-winger (8)
4 Heart of a nuclear reactor? (4)
5 Very fine drink going round the circuit (4-2)
6 In the chalk, Alice discovered a chemical (6)
7 Weight-y man? (4)
10 Polly got about, using many languages (8)
12 Bored, by the sound of it, in the kitchen which must be very tiring (8)
14 Permission to begin something – motorists go on it (5,5)
16 Look at cur from monitoring organisation (8)
17 Disturbing bird with fish (8)
19 Small Scotch according to hired mourner (6)

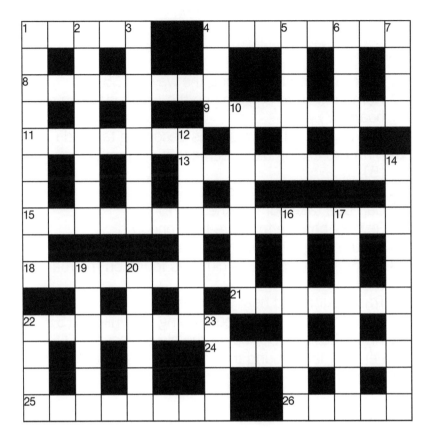

20 New money father had from Phoenician princess (6)

22 Second gear for take-off (4)

23 Record I see, say, or poem (4)

ACROSS

1 Direct confrontation along the way (4-2,5)
7 Number said to be going on the upper platform on board (7)
8 Dull ringing sound when it is becoming tangled (7)
10 Man expressing disagreement in eastern church (5)
11 Bar, but China's not troubled (9)
12 Can Dee take our frankness? (7)
14 Reveals change for more than one (7)
15 Secure long talk about disease (7)
18 Bounder in royal lady's clutches found on the road (7)
20 Trail a cur round near the joint (9)
21 More than ten go to sleep having nap initially (5)
22 Timer that is designed for the old professors (7)
23 Perfectly lazily round the middle of the Weald (7)
24 Fractionally lower figure (11)

DOWN

1 Instrument with ring attached, it's the main weapon! (7)
2 It doesn't make a sound when dropped (5)
3 One who resists work, a model (7)
4 Scope for boxers (7)
5 Against 104 with another 99 who were not in favour of citizenship (9)
6 More than one lock? (7)
7 Adieu (6,5)
9 Fellow only half behaving in a polite manner (11)
13 Protest at the article I put on (9)
16 Felix had the main beam (7)
17 Sweet boy (7)
18 Green man in a tram crash (7)

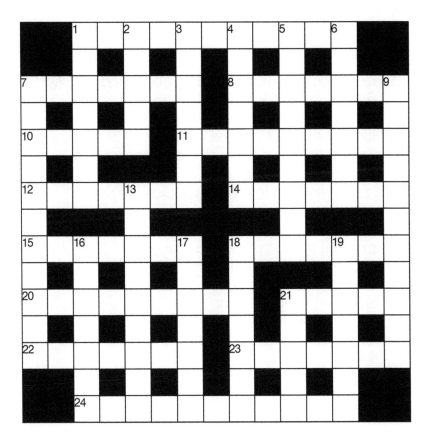

19 Bobby's very bright light? (7)
21 Stayed and spoke at length (5)

ACROSS

1 He carried out reforms involving beer and petrol (6,4)
9 A way the old can show complaint (4)
10 Hunt for a drink? Just the opposite (7-3)
11 Klaus seen going round a foreign capital (6)
12 No current source of light (7)
15 A tug in a storm in the West Indies (7)
16 At festive occasions a journalist is treated (5)
17 As a result a work unit gains nothing (4)
18 I'm going round in reverse in car (4)
19 No banker would credit it (5)
21 Colonist gets letters sent out (7)
22 Review on thug's weapon (7)
24 It holds wine for a service in church (6)
27 Red Admiral flutters around on the football field (4,6)
28 Bringer of love and life? (4)
29 Sewer join takes strain (10)

DOWN

2 Picks a spot for recreation (4)
3 With the organ study over, got paid employment (6)
4 Affected with slight insanity (7)
5 Produce a work of art from scratch (4)
6 Country boy holds a map (7)
7 Taking another person's life in one's hands (10)
8 Compensation required for port area in ruins (10)
12 Tasty dish, or picture of one? (10)
13 The late shift? (10)
14 Straighten robes, like a judge (5)
15 In a way age is some protection (5)
19 Abandons wastelands (7)

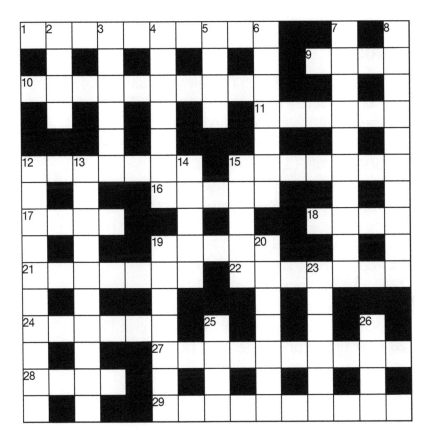

20 It doesn't normally contain mother's ruin (7)
23 One who cares is easily hurt (6)
25 Mountain ash? (4)
26 A failure as a teacher (4)

23

ACROSS

1 Pirate's underclothes horribly vile, right? (4,4,6)
9 Comparatively crazy row after club (7)
10 Flies perhaps in separate groups (7)
11 Odd of us to see mysterious craft (4)
12 Share profit (10)
14 Ingratiating, sergeant-major with his employer (6)
15 Appropriate vehicle again hired out (8)
17 He's willing to dispose of his effects (8)
18 Careless about girls (6)
21 Poet's utterances have value (10)
22 Doubly nervous, so bitten? (4)
24 Show teeth – put back bleeding molar (7)
25 With delicate leg, Antonia showing chic (7)
26 A bit blue round finger-joint (4,3,7)

DOWN

1 Works for party on Sunday (7)
2 Never antisocial work in this spell in army (8,7)
3 Fall sick after judge gives prison term (4)
4 Some abhor nettle – it stings (6)
5 Needlewomen's pains? (8)
6 Long leases available in US city (3,7)
7 Outcry over gospel! (11,4)
8 Agree, since enraptured (6)
13 Abroad, mass movement requires diplomat (10)
16 Run out of horror mag edited in wicked city (8)
17 Drawing fee, put to earnings (6)
19 Cover girl has secret passion (7)
20 Barely manage to run (6)
23 Choice of courses for people going to university (4)

ACROSS

1 Californian banker makes entreaty after Eucharist (10)
6 Crack shot (4)
10 Carol may not embrace Henry (5)
11 Apply oneself anew to study costume (9)
12 Quickly produced two slices of meat (4-4)
13 A multitude returning from Indian state (5)
15 Works to disclose division of unknown quantity (7)
17 A famous writer? The devil it is! (7)
19 Essay about ancient drama (7)
21 Left-wing video exposing excessive formality (3,4)
22 Urge to see one's breakfast cooking? (3,2)
24 Use a filter again to check (8)
27 Where to apply cosmetic varnish pronto (2,3,4)
28 A couple needing support (5)
29 Some pupils work industriously in class (4)
30 One-metre gable causing an obstruction (10)

DOWN

1 Fire and plunder (4)
2 Take steps to provide tea for three (3-3-3)
3 Make trouble after current set-back (3,2)
4 Secular novice in crude accommodation (7)
5 Tory leader criticised for being outmanoeuvred (7)
7 Seen to be upset about many basic requirements (5)
8 Expert ex-teacher (4,6)
9 Given credit for having made headway (8)
14 Out of trouble whilst sailing past south west Holland (3,3,4)
16 A bloomer no dealer made (8)
18 I created a disturbance to cause destruction (9)
20 CID to carry weapons on board ship (4-3)

21 Determination to find another answer (7)
23 Managed to travel over 100mph (3,2)
25 Butler and bishop meet one religious leader (5)
26 Beat the unbeatable (4)

ACROSS

1 Rifles taking a back seat (5)
4 The guards going out with one's girls? (9)
8 Bid for cash-box that does not open (5)
9 Ignorant, having tried to discard knowledge (9)
11 Nose out of joint for ages (4)
12 Design square factory (5)
13 Fish spear (4)
16 Inconsistent quality of ceilings, all so different (13)
19 Sigmund's close catchers making unintentional errors (8,5)
20 Rolling peas in church recess (4)
22 Couple to marry (5)
23 Change was roughly one penny short (4)
26 Odd, perhaps, to include going wrong in bold action (7-2)
27 Difficult, some say, to get hospital well-ventilated (5)
28 Stroll off like Lady Macbeth (9)
29 But is not Harris's river! (5)

DOWN

1 Album for the autumn (5-4)
2 Detestable attack (9)
3 Slave once almost got up invigorated (4)
4 Fitting twin lights for extra warmth (6,7)
5 Try to listen (4)
6 The doldrums, a bit of a rotten nuisance (5)
7 Grass edges trimmed (5)
10 The grandfather to face Jarndyce v Jarndyce? (8,5)
14 Dashing young fellow, a swordsman (5)
15 Clear grassland (5)
17 Once, where list was amended (9)
18 Musical character looked alert (5-4)

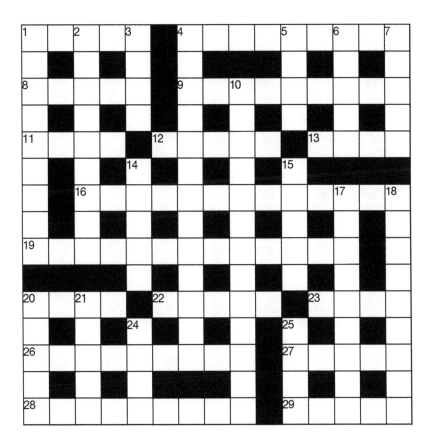

20 Range of *Danse Macabre*? (5)
21 Swell certain to grip top of glove (5)
24 Strand, from west, is quiet (4)
25 Scrap this holiday? (4)

26

ACROSS

1 They may be grating, but they are conservation minded (8)
5 Put much effort into accommodating voters (6)
9 When he plays he keeps stopping (8)
10 Found the French male in a strong position (6)
12 The Prime Minister lets go and goes to pieces (9)
13 Division in Croatia (5)
14 A young attendant brought to book? (4)
16 Inspired article put back or employed (7)
19 Tells of churchmen being decapitated (7)
21 Opposed to some entrant in the big race (4)
24 The rogue will do badly (5)
25 A fast mover's chores are well-organised (9)
27 One way to cook second-rate produce (6)
28 Preparing a hot meal (8)
29 No-one thanks right back for any allowance made (6)
30 Dash impressed the egghead (8)

DOWN

1 Cast off – it's very muddy (6)
2 When students can revel in their scruffy clothing? (3-3)
3 Places around the north building boats (5)
4 Dealing with bank refund (7)
6 Entrance for lorries? (9)
7 Better in an open-air school? (8)
8 There's a steady drift at day's end (8)
11 A girl in overalls (4)
15 Tasty morsel served in pots at a get-together (9)
17 Upset over prohibition on the bicycle (8)
18 Affable country person without money (8)
20 The kind to arrange things (4)

21 Bill's found a number are of some importance (7)
22 A fleshy-leafed plant or tree (6)
23 Spare silver put into a pool (6)
26 One-man women (5)

27

ACROSS

1 Recoil now that the milder weather has returned? (6,4)
6 In a dreadful state (4)
10 Set sail without a meal (5)
11 A lady to suit you? (9)
12 Gurgling sound coming from southern queen by the Spanish church (7)
13 Dog's tip (7)
14 The colour of Ireland? (7,5)
18 Stop, ended confusion about engineers when it was seized for military use (12)
21 Turn round and rue disastrous upbringing (7)
23 Justification for a poor specimen (7)
24 Fragmentary bit of 10 (9)
25 After a short attempt, has to remove the rubbish (5)
26 Seat made out of bristle (4)
27 Some defence used to tie a game (10)

DOWN

1 A little soda-water produces a sensation (6)
2 Exit hurriedly when dismissed (3,3)
3 All-out order for pints (2,4,8)
4 Ruined beer, Dutch variety (9)
5 Companion with little devil, the little monkey (5)
7 One who gets to grips with his opponents (8)
8 Asking Desmond, before one, to make a call (8)
9 One who is not still in journalism (6,8)
15 Willingly permit it to remain unploughed (3,6)
16 Soundly breaks the spirit (8)
17 Suddenly appearing to be swallowed up in otorhinolaryngology shortly (8)
19 Boy following Henry's Catherine (6)
20 Fruity content of Caerphilly cheese (6)
22 Chieftain always going round Middle East (5)

28

ACROSS

7 Attack main site of obsolete London power station (9)
8 Easily shattered by loud abuse (5)
10 Joined in, without being searched (8)
11 Run or climb up it (6)
12 Rough deal for one loved by Zeus (4)
13 The way the world goes round (8)
15 X-ray penetration? (7)
17 Random attempt by a snooker player? (3-4)
20 He appreciates the exquisite tea these provide (8)
22 A mild imprecation – here's an example (4)
25 The lowest form of birds (6)
26 What's behind China preparing for new conflict? (8)
27 Where a washer is always available (2,3)
28 Drink before business – it's no joke without it (9)

DOWN

1 Can't you be done for drink driving when on this vehicle? (5)
2 Building fast (6)
3 Go to barn to mix animal food? (4-4)
4 Ground prepared for development? (7)
5 They're boring quarrels about publicity (8)
6 Not to be made light of (9)
9 Sign for more (4)
14 A French river bore (9)
16 Sacked, no doubt (2,3,3)
18 Arms can end or cause trouble (8)
19 For sure construction contains iron (7)
21 Language used in the Upper Senate (4)
23 Lots follow second test (6)
24 Being stupid, Annie gets confused (5)

29

ACROSS

1 Put jacket on to follow pioneer (5-6)
9 Author, say, who attracts the punters (9)
10 Richard is in poor condition (5)
11 Bird was first to be given a name (6)
12 Cleaner fuel, of a dark grey colour (8)
13 No d-drink? Here's a little (6)
15 Drunk, cause inn trouble (8)
18 Signalling one's getting tired? (8)
19 A sign twins are due next month (6)
21 Get actor to represent rural worker (8)
23 River rose, for example (6)
26 Failure is nearer losing head (5)
27 Violent argument about one that flies in a gale (5,4)
28 Delights in a dance to which partners are specially invited (6,5)

DOWN

1 In fact, I bet Angus is a Highlander (7)
2 A fight joined roughly (5)
3 Being clumsy felling trees (9)
4 Enjoy being similar (4)
5 When start is due, but nothing's on time (4,4)
6 The police reflect on use of this gun (5)
7 By which I mean I might be replaced by the monarch? (5,2)
8 Con shore quizzically from ship (8)
14 Large woman: it's Agnes in disguise (8)
16 Worker with horses is a steady chap (9)
17 Ignorant of poetry? (8)
18 Particular skill of university department? (7)
20 Excess of waves – tie up (7)
22 Fall sick touring Puerto Rico for a month (5)

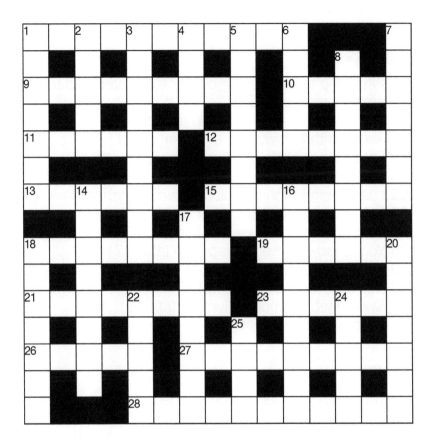

24 Your answer to this clue won't be right (5)
25 Manage company on exercise (4)

30

ACROSS

1 What one tells travelling builder to be prepared for army discipline (4-5)
6 Exemplary healer induced to return (5)
9 About to thrash worker for calling aloud (7)
10 Foolishly maintain oriental is without vitality (9)
11 Daughter is to relax following illness (7)
12 I have permission to include German symbolism (7)
13 CID officer is no dandy (5-7,3)
18 French philosopher died in torment? Rubbish! (7)
20 Young lady, I have to prepare a letter (7)
22 Sid, Ed and I went mad when treated scornfully (9)
23 Fish for the landlord's lady? (7)
24 Sweetened alcohol is divine in trifle (5)
25 Youth generates disruption (9)

DOWN

1 Improved after being reprimanded (6,2)
2 The cleaner has children with irresistible appeal (8)
3 Lawyer admits damage caused by Indian custom (6)
4 Eventually played at the correct tempo (2,4)
5 Ally is to be used in the sovereign's service (8)
6 Contemplate having friend around to make corrections (8)
7 Socialite scoffed in discussion (6)
8 Probably £51,000 needed by English cathedral (6)
14 No male interrupts mass meeting as a rule (8)
15 Linguist demands "Can I come in at the end?" (8)
16 Principal occupation for the railway company? (4,4)
17 Uncalled-for advice to the overindulgent (8)
18 Edward returned pipe to get discount (6)
19 Frustrated by seeing woman in father's embrace (6)

20 Frenchwoman forced to accommodate a Frenchman (6)

21 A scene set by Roman dramatist (6)

31

ACROSS

1 Legal charges? (11)
8 The planting of trees in front of official premises (11)
11 Argonaut said to be mutinous (4)
12 Record notice (4)
13 Having sent in wrong key is really serious (7)
15 A teller of stories after following soldiers (7)
16 Give way with little hesitation – it's wiser! (5)
17 The expedition set off (4)
18 Deny oneself unflinchingly (4)
19 Respond and create endless agitation (5)
21 Gun turned on a rebel leader as ordered (7)
22 One should require no additional luggage (4-3)
23 Small type – that's material (4)
26 Quiet English river, quite unpolluted (4)
27 See printers working out schemes (11)
28 A suggestion of professional standing (11)

DOWN

2 Duck in Greek island sounds like a dove! (4)
3 There's no point in advising economy (7)
4 Con a diligent worker – single (4)
5 He speaks in tone that relaxes initially (7)
6 The day-centre (4)
7 An artist whose output is not large (11)
8 Cheap drink once fashionable with women (11)
9 "Amour" stands for ruin for this fortune-teller (11)
10 The sportsman may well get ahead (11)
14 A consumer of some taste – a terse fellow (5)
15 Come to a stretch of water (5)
19 Use pair bonding to give lift (5,2)
20 Person travelling to ancient city first (7)
24 The knot tier shown up (4)

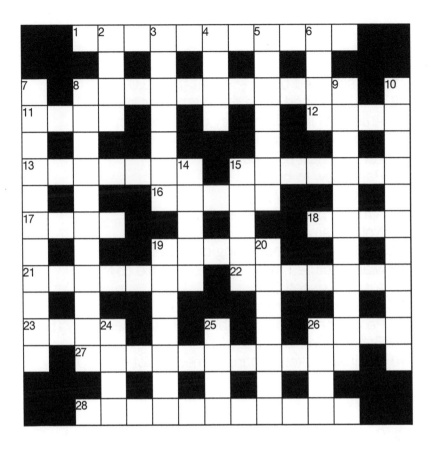

25 Pop in a steamer and they'll be health-giving (4)
26 Ridiculous pose struck by South Americans (4)

32

ACROSS

1 Not schooled badly – repeat that (10)
6 A little inclined to be apologetic, but game (4)
10 Artist making top military officer corrupt (5)
11 Men met and organised alteration (9)
12 Left the next-door party (8)
13 Page slow to bring coat (5)
15 Finish off, do! (7)
17 Aimless perhaps, yet earth-moving (7)
19 Note sharp pain can be trying (7)
21 Taking a pen and writing of a Greek god (7)
22 Manufactured food – finished article (5)
24 A sticky sweet! (8)
27 A state of unconsciousness (9)
28 People having made a bloomer start hesitantly (5)
29 Fish trodden underfoot (4)
30 Manual worker creating a mess? Not on! (10)

DOWN

1 Go slowly in the fast lane in cheeky fashion (4)
2 With "green" make-up a girl's content, that's the size of it (9)
3 Coachwork is his speciality! (5)
4 Understand how to turn assets into cash (7)
5 Attic hero uses the revised version (7)
7 Dramatic music (5)
8 Finding more buyers as a market trader? (10)
9 Taking on a dunderhead, work into shape (8)
14 Crawlers inspected possibly about a quarter (10)
16 Held like a small child, which is revolting (2,2,4)
18 Joggers – strange men! Many love turning in to the Court of Sessions (9)
20 To harass a conservationist body would be brave (7)

21 Youth in trouble needed a knightly champion (7)
23 Charming words put into letters (5)
25 Turn of phrase – the same one a medico backs (5)
26 Avoid attention (4)

33

ACROSS

1 Be unsuccessful in crossing the frozen surface? (4,7)
7 Regretfully captured the flighty creature (5)
8 Frightened as we overturned the vehicle (9)
10 Shade over our heads (3-4)
11 Alone it could have produced high spirits (7)
12 Endlessly harp on the French composer (5)
13 Indoctrinate or clear the head? (9)
16 Sent mates round in an official enquiry (5,4)
18 Clown with a drink (5)
19 Old soldier's car? (7)
22 Produce an eviction order? (4,3)
23 Frank runs before nine to lady on board (9)
24 Boy I had inclined to fear (5)
25 Blinder produced by one puffing a cigarette? (11)

DOWN

1 Soft hairy sort of flowering shrub (9)
2 Little goes right for golfer Gene (7)
3 Possible to find small amount before island uprising (9)
4 Magistrate needing a ruff (5)
5 Transport not used to go downtown? (2-5)
6 One o'clock nymph (5)
7 Like emotional people, can be transported without difficulty (6,5)
9 Sympathetic sort listen to Edward (4-7)
14 Against poisonous substance or just neutralising it? (9)
15 Fasten chap to last runner in relay-race (9)
17 Blow for man, commander backing company (7)
18 Tree cut haphazardly with a surgical instrument (7)
20 Bull said to be found at the base of a column (5)
21 Senor turned out to be Scandinavian (5)

34

ACROSS

1 When guns are effectively fired in anger, perhaps? (2,5)
5 Dishing out for a party (7)
9 It's to do with good breeding (7)
10 Wood that is metal to start with (7)
11 The poor may find it accommodating (9)
12 Cheese made with some French backing in Goa (5)
13 Port one gets in casks (5)
15 Fair distribution of beer to all (9)
17 Some French married, but didn't expect to be happy (9)
19 Don't take time off (5)
22 Start to fight (3-2)
23 Port of fine quality (9)
25 Possibly a Sûreté stiff! (7)
26 Seem upset about flag signal (7)
27 Rugby player is crafty one of pair (3-4)
28 Girl with enthusiasm for the cloth (7)

DOWN

1 In-law embracing divorcee? That's not quite right (7)
2 Treatment received by troops losing Turkish capital (7)
3 Man in the orchestra gives Beethoven's choral symphony (5)
4 Meet in French bar (9)
5 Brush a fur coat (5)
6 Introductory speech, perhaps (9)
7 I'd burst out when upset (7)
8 Out of range of French explosive device (7)
14 Propose a broadcast on the first of August – a serial drama (4,5)

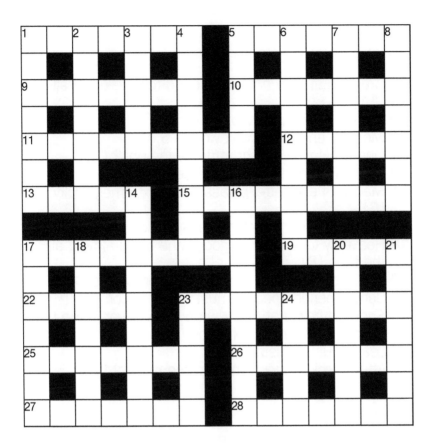

16 One fond of the girls put damsel in a turmoil (6,3)
17 Hell for a Welshman at his mother's side (7)
18 Please pay in full (7)
20 Yet a cricketer is not out to improve his (7)
21 Could be set near China, for example (7)
23 People aren't wanted on this board (5)
24 How bread's gone up! (5)

35

ACROSS

1 Crack, that may naturally herald terrible downfall (11)
10 Drink with Bishop before a dance (5)
11 Men driven mad? Don't worry! (5,4)
12 One making compact refrigeration unit? (9)
13 Butterfly spends minute in deep sleep (5)
14 Matter of etiquette, pleasant but extremely tricky (6)
16 Sort of solid and lacking sensual desire (8)
18 Heavenly to find some good wine there almost all the time (8)
20 Ran around always getting savagely criticised (6)
23 School periods people must agree to come to (5)
24 Snowfall heavy at first – wrap a bedcover round (9)
26 People admitting to joint title (9)
27 Leaps out by mistake (5)
28 After check, announcing replacement (11)

DOWN

2 Being almost merciful (5)
3 Very close attention given in the home (7)
4 Sternest chap? No way (6)
5 Enveloping garment, with or without top (5-3)
6 A price cut to shift fruit (7)
7 Prejudice, before becoming pregnant (13)
8 More cash than this needed to make pony mine? (3,5)
9 Lent uniform for exam (8,5)
15 Firm present books, orderly and logical (8)
17 Battle caused harm, not a doubt (8)
19 Save up for book (7)
21 Flyer found part of tree hindrance (7)
22 Covering exercise in trailer (6)
25 In tin, half pork and poultry (5)

36

ACROSS

1 A blooming easy life (3,2,5)
6 Many a member is effeminate (4)
9 Make allusions, anyway (5)
10 What arsonists did to sections of Trieste (3,4,2)
12 Obvious means one used to prove one's innocence (5,4,4)
14 A doctor entered no information on hormone (8)
15 Aim to make a protest (6)
17 Humiliated a retired Anglo-Saxon (6)
19 Ideal breakfast for a jailbird (8)
21 Together, notwithstanding (2,3,4,4)
24 Remain loyal – to one's religion (4,5)
25 A couple of males needing capital (5)
26 Anything but a quiet meal (4)
27 Type of car to alarm some on return (10)

DOWN

1 Poet is utterly excluded (4)
2 Vandalised by footballers caught in the act (7)
3 Think only of others, yet offend others (6,7)
4 He watches old bishop preceding acolyte (8)
5 Consumed some meat, endive and potato (5)
7 To feel fury after greeting is mean (7)
8 Attributes valued by estate agents (10)
11 Single Pole of inferior rank becomes rebellious (13)
13 Barmy family may be a hazard (6,4)
16 How steam is produced? Rather! (8)
18 A lady of many parts (7)
20 Finding me in drab accommodation is romantic (7)
22 Labour leader leaves a country house in Spain (5)
23 Crack under the strain and speak sharply (4)

37

ACROSS

1 Joe outlined arm movement in love play (5,3,6)
9 Social climber at university receives shock (7)
10 A canapé prepared as a cure-all (7)
11 This is not repeated in a concerto (4)
12 Parts of pub serving loaf-sticks? (6,4)
14 Fish not taken originally in British water (6)
15 Sharp drops in pollution (4,4)
17 Turkish blade swings it, I scram! (8)
18 Note area of smallest possible numbers (6)
21 Anticipation of preferred alternative to healing (10)
22 Small coin of Indian nation (4)
24 Girl, given new title, gets first-class return (7)
25 Issue English chap devoured (7)
26 In theory, he is no prankster (9,5)

DOWN

1 Hoarsely loud, caucus rhyme (7)
2 MD putting out court disclaimer (7,8)
3 Duck-eggs perhaps, long seen in cricket ground (4)
4 Central pair leave the swimming race (6)
5 Jack not finishing piano arrangement of *Camellia* (8)
6 Sell iodine extract for protection of bats (7,3)
7 One showing stress at end of sentence (11,4)
8 Standard disciple of parish priest (6)
13 Cooked pies intact, germ free (10)
16 From Parma, it's smoked beef (8)
17 Flexible composer accepts lire (6)
19 No bread for him in his game (7)
20 Ancient old boy putting up wine-shop (6)
23 Had Jerusalem initially in mind as destination for pilgrimage (4)

38

ACROSS

1 Rejects and scoffs at make-up (5,3)
5 A good man got into debt when laid up (6)
9 Till the cows come home nevertheless! (8)
10 Aims to get well? (6)
11 Sits with reel spinning without wearying of it (8)
12 Part after exchanging a quiet word (6)
14 They're under pressure to provide a weather-forecast (10)
18 The ministry defector, admitting nothing, left (10)
22 This man's mud-slinging in consequence (6)
23 At home alone with a good book that's really saucy (8)
24 Set free to follow a relative (6)
25 Urge turning around in trains with caution (8)
26 Issue some schemer generally raises (6)
27 Get aid at getting organisation wound up (8)

DOWN

1 A man surrounded by animals – does (6)
2 Drink if apprehensive about blunder (6)
3 A model politician will be in Cheshire town (6)
4 Prevents everyone going into the woods (10)
6 Warn theatre characters over a point (8)
7 Stroll across – it's child's play (8)
8 Do without to give to others (8)
13 Brooding about nurse with foreboding (10)
15 Rock-bottom price? (4,4)
16 Start with the guys caught in advance (8)
17 Carol holds colour to be limiting (8)
19 Direction should be looked for (6)
20 A number perhaps aren't absorbed (6)
21 Given some support, didn't quit (6)

39

ACROSS

1 My code has been cracked – it should amuse you (6)
4 Does it have a souped-up engine for racing? (5-3)
10 Hospital doctor's a recorder (9)
11 Imitate cold operatic role first (5)
12 After a new cathedral church for the Pope St John (7)
13 Another tree in the bunch had to be irrigated (7)
14 Gritty Scot! (5)
15 Battle controversy (8)
18 Girl in the orchestra with a coloured handkerchief (8)
20 In composition, four of the quintet rallied (5)
23 Make a incision removing lice from dead skin (7)
25 A spiteful woman about to steal a tumbler (7)
26 Thanks Kentucky cheerleader included for making it sticky (5)
27 Sum is made hesitantly on this machine! (9)
28 Quadruple? (8)
29 Way of communicating a proverb (6)

DOWN

1 Negligent being without a vehicle about start of Easter (8)
2 Margaret had a weighty unit of explosive power (7)
3 Another story in the act was ruined (9)
5 Having a fling in politics? (8,1,5)
6 Army chief encountered heavenly body (5)
7 It's material that the saloon is carrying the doctor in charge (7)
8 Move backwards when about to give up (6)
9 Surpassing others in this meditation (14)
16 Strictly till early revolution (9)

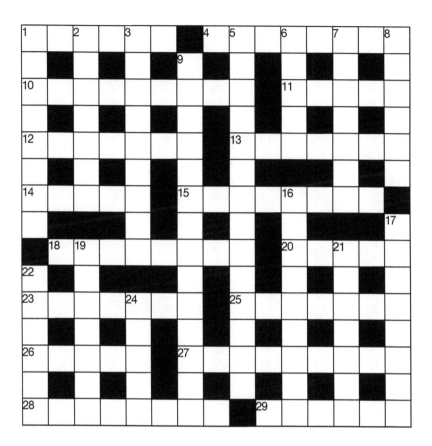

17 Took chief officer on River Dee, say (8)
19 It is alkaline and makes the worker bitter (7)
21 Keep tabs round a company making hot sauce (7)
22 Duck coming from Tresco (6)
24 Rodent or shy bear was reported (5)

40

ACROSS

1 Closely fought embroidery competitions? (6,7)
10 Above and just behind the clock (7)
11 To economise is of no avail (7)
12 Quiet place for entertainment (4)
13 A mouthful of water (5)
14 It can't be passed in silence (4)
17 Is stout perhaps, so doesn't dance (4,3)
18 Accomplished young woman in Irish county set (7)
19 Has prep to revise, maybe (7)
22 Time taken by secretary? (7)
24 Vain and lazy (4)
25 Blazing aloud with anger (5)
26 Business unlikely to go into liquidation? (4)
29 He may be a master of form (7)
30 It's funny, there's nothing in the box (7)
31 Rather old to be harnessing a horse? (7,2,1,3)

DOWN

2 Graceful, with a gentle styling (7)
3 Hearing of Troy's fall, she took no action (4)
4 One constituent of fire may be oxygen, for example (7)
5 With only a fag-end Edward was up against it (7)
6 They may be used to take pot-shots (4)
7 Time for settling scores? (7)
8 They're of cardinal importance – for dividers? (7,6)
9 Setting up in business (13)
15 The result of a summer's work? (5)
16 Silly Annie is upset (5)
20 Let go of a catch (7)
21 Colouring when second offence is detailed (7)
22 Hide in Africa (7)
23 Travel to new oil capital (7)

27 A very small amount for the time of year (4)
28 Professional on a sailing vessel (4)

41

ACROSS

1 Growing concern following a beastly takeover (6,4)
6 Naval port (4)
10 A spice endlessly used in savoury food (5)
11 Able perhaps to occupy jar cleaner (9)
12 To put in reserve team after tea's unusual (3,5)
13 Encourages when about to gamble (5)
15 Continue to offer support (7)
17 In Lewisham poor folk must share a washer (7)
19 Neat, and possibly rather slow (7)
21 Making a note on evidence that's to go over again (7)
22 A quarter say are doubtful (5)
24 Jocular talk which could get naughty in time (8)
27 Cook cut a liver in shreds. It's so beneficial (9)
28 Overcharges men on the board (5)
29 A girl using Spanish and French articles (4)
30 The custodian in control – one who is invariably calm (4,6)

DOWN

1 A fish or seaweed extract (4)
2 Once forced to join up, had real impact (9)
3 The capital of a couple of hundred big guns (5)
4 Make way (7)
5 Activists' new roster absorbing the unit (7)
7 Finding bearings after a time, get out (5)
8 Insures hides (5,5)
9 A form of support many a worker is wearing (8)
14 Writer putting money into very large car – spacious (5,5)
16 Irregular ban, moral though it may be (8)
18 Cast for the amusement of youngsters? (9)
20 Dropping in the main (3-4)

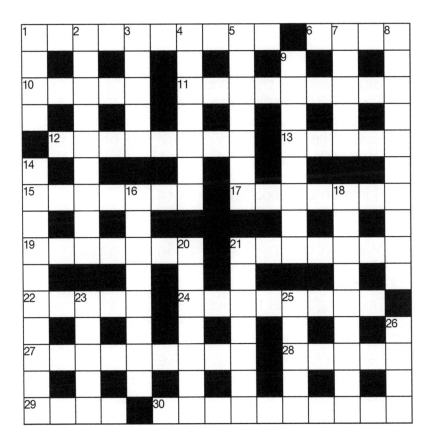

21 He'd read about an auburn-haired woman (7)

23 Opposing the top man a Latin can be articulate! (5)

25 Only the patient will attract her attention (5)

26 The person working for some good cause regularly (4)

42

ACROSS

1 He's afraid of a crowd rioting (6)
4 Easy task to knock to ground (4-4)
9 Mercilessly attack wise man about Bible (6)
10 Eastern hemisphere only in ancient globe (3,5)
12 For learning, look to engineers (4)
13 Dishonest trader in garden material? (5)
14 Summon just about everybody (4)
17 Single-mindedness required of Eurostar driver? (6,6)
20 Massage, one might say, that Shylock wanted (5,2,5)
23 Burden boy carries round (4)
24 Tail off right after finishing line (5)
25 Damage limb – going to hospital (4)
28 Be old now, sadly, needing fresh vigour (3,5)
29 Sell cure for the *Three Blind Mice*? (6)
30 *1 across* work gets annoyingly up one's nose (3,5)
31 Hordes travel to this holiday island (6)

DOWN

1 Randomly choose actors – plenty (4,4)
2 Uncertain signal to arena (8)
3 Fashion strong emotion (4)
5 Not fair – client could turn nasty (4,8)
6 Start to hear wise old bird cry (4)
7 Severn – a little bore in the spring (6)
8 Have lots of shots at cryptic puzzle (6)
11 Paradise is in the sky? My word! (7,5)
15 Feel depressed, in bowels of ship? (5)
16 Gosh! No end of fun in island (5)
18 Agile lad's extraordinary help with case (5,3)
19 Quiet walks to abattoir (8)
21 Bird round lake is quail (6)

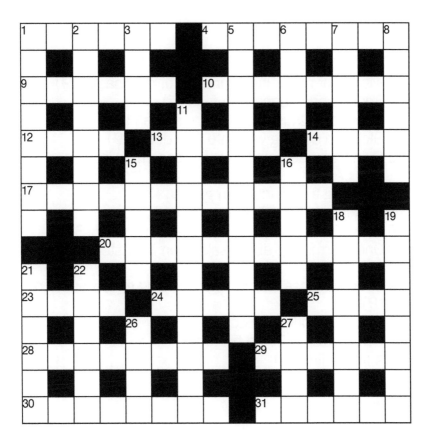

22 Girl takes route to Irish county (6)
26 Hint – you're reading it (4)
27 Little woman's wager with Henry (4)

43

ACROSS

1 Means of measuring contents of dirty sack? (9)
6 Sounds not pleasant to face (5)
9 Firm's to dismiss Russian horseman (7)
10 Skilful in dealing with info and debts (9)
11 Ruining by demolition work – becoming hardened to it (7)
12 Climbing-frame found in garden (7)
13 Winning combination in court (4,3,3,5)
18 Yet we're possibly found in the churchyard (3-4)
20 One murmuring about salesman in Eastern Region (7)
22 Becoming less severe when yielding to compassion (9)
23 Resisted work, puzzled (7)
24 Come second in the hill race? (3,2)
25 A trashy line (9)

DOWN

1 Youth leader Bill had night out sailing (8)
2 Is rude strangely and hesitantly with the matter remaining (8)
3 Rascal, one with seafood (6)
4 Clue not left for blackening (6)
5 Ruler converts tons of capital (8)
6 Ray spends short time on the side of the ship (8)
7 Some forms of fish? (6)
8 Councillor one's repeatedly followed during the emergency (6)
14 Begin suddenly to jump out of bed (6,2)
15 Peg, one found in home that's the smallest (8)
16 Wasn't one working with the tool? (5-3)
17 Larry, he'd removed the armorial bearings (8)
18 Ball Kerry spun was empty (6)

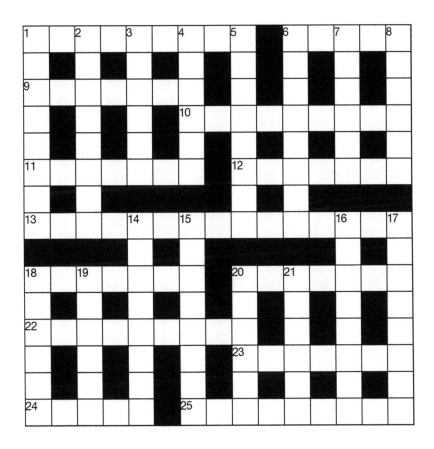

19 Flag on the carpet (6)
20 Rex and I go to the old city during the austerity (6)
21 Handles the fruit (6)

44

ACROSS

1 To relieve tension, hear recital performed (5,3,3)
7 Keep on being cheeky about little relative (7)
8 A small quantity of Latin? (7)
10 Soldiers returned, having no way settled to sleep (5)
11 No government supporter (9)
12 Some apprentice disgracefully led astray (7)
14 Perhaps English beach (7)
15 About to drink, to interrupt his spasms (7)
18 Curse pet with cowed air (7)
20 Causing annoyance by clumsiness? (9)
21 Blow oxygen with relish (5)
22 Point to good book, a typical example (7)
23 Adolescent period before one makes a score? (7)
24 So, man, hatter made you this? (3-1-7)

DOWN

1 Vehicle left – under cover here? (3,4)
2 Authoritative pronouncement from the dictionary (5)
3 Tedious routine? Come down to this county (7)
4 When these books are in service, sing praises (7)
5 A tonic did wonders for this craving (9)
6 Like grandpa in chair, or youngster playing music? (7)
7 Doorman takes home steak (11)
9 Pantomime gets the bird (6,5)
13 Space for tennis? Hold trial here (9)
16 Plausible arguer makes a Conservative's suit fall apart (7)
17 Trembles and smashes (7)
18 Meal excellent – ate out (4,3)
19 Praised for beating depression (7)
21 Big fireplace, we hear (5)

45

ACROSS

1 & 5 Descriptive of a wild cheetah? (4,3,7)
9 Give a party a new constitution, perhaps (7)
10 Display anger when having a brush with someone (7)
11 Locks controller (9)
12 It's socially unacceptable in a class debate (5)
13 & 15 Just twice is correct (5,3,6)
17 Elaborate metal work to stop a bit of play (9)
19 The Spanish weapon involved in the movement of arms (5)
22 She's a vessel in the drink (5)
23 Trial trials (4,5)
25 What it means to a barman (7)
26 Sort of roll made with herb and an American stuffing (7)
27 A help or hindrance in the works (7)
28 Don't stop, although a person's upset (5,2)

DOWN

1 & 17 Extra information provided from more remote army detachments (7,7)
2 Making one's name as a writer (7)
3 Little things to put in a manuscript (5)
4 Not a unique type of bridge (9)
5 Untrue statement about an essential part of one's diet (5)
6 Increase support to control violence (9)
7 Poor cut of rock formation (7)
8 Not a galley, but may be found in one (7)
14 Pacific islander is a man with a tan, perhaps (9)
16 Prepares for a costume party? (7,2)
17 See *1 down*
18 Cosmetic surgery's result concealed by mother (7)

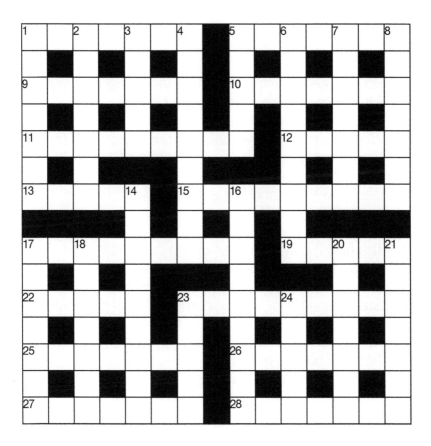

20 Public vehicle licence (3,4)
21 The Navy get under way in short film (7)
23 Singer with half a score gets nothing right (5)
24 Vessel is said to be *en voyage* (5)

46

ACROSS

1 How someone who was laden had influence? (7,6)
7 Excited to see the man put out (3,2)
8 Put in new order for back boiler (9)
9 Where one may hear the sound of cows away from the mountains (7)
10 Shellfish for sailor on his own (7)
11 Danny, disheartened, is unwell going round the charming scene (5)
12 Burglar – or comedian? (9)
14 The first flighty character at the controls? (4,5)
17 Bill and he had continued giving pain (5)
19 Saying it's a grape I'm making a mess of (7)
21 Grab me violently, taking nothing during the trade ban (7)
22 As pointed out in New Zealand perhaps (9)
23 Tie up a bundle of hay (5)
24 Very old retired bishop's greeting? (4,4,2,3)

DOWN

1 Remove something, a method to shorten at the beginning (3,4)
2 Artist, help a different artist (7)
3 Girl, Heidi, an Austrian in hiding (5)
4 Set aside a distinctive characteristic (7)
5 A French partner in the union going round the armoury (7)
6 Suddenly understand money is losing its value (3,5,5)
7 Difficult to find place to get money from (4-2-3-4)
8 Another arid state is basic (7)
13 Being naive, he left without a suit (7)
15 Wooden prop placed on the cheese (7)
16 Piece about monkey on the wall (7)

17 From USA, Burt brought a strawberry tree (7)
18 Being hairy might suit her! (7)
20 Lady's title from two different mothers (5)

47

ACROSS

1 Letters to a girl in uniform giving directions? (9)
9 A Moor has to return a greeting (7)
10 Those keeping count may well get crosser (7)
11 Standard forms to state date of birth (7)
12 A merry celebration for vegetarians only? (9)
14 Reliable person turning to a silly eccentric (8)
15 Warning a French minor (6)
17 A number leave no doubt of blame (7)
20 Rambling royal letters go on and on (6)
23 Tides can vary to a certain extent (8)
25 Director making a note on storage furniture (9)
26 Suffer when in the red – stretched (7)
27 Go down and open one quietly (7)
28 There's not now a brochure to bring out (7)
29 Outrage of bag, say, taken in to cause vexation (9)

DOWN

2 Rank of relative requiring an attendant (7)
3 Get mad with some trader, angered beyond endurance (7)
4 Contumacious minister turned in by himself (8)
5 A salad with excessively dull content (6)
6 Manufacturer producing only the most basic wear (9)
7 European dogs' home (7)
8 It's cheapest frequently on the North Sea coast (9)
13 Lads get upset about a girl being cut (7)
15 A round end is quite wrong, that's plain (9)
16 Quarrel a lot? Rubbish! (9)
18 One may well upbraid the salesman, a traveller (8)
19 Points to some duck grass (7)
21 Role almost totally absorbing new star of the stage (7)

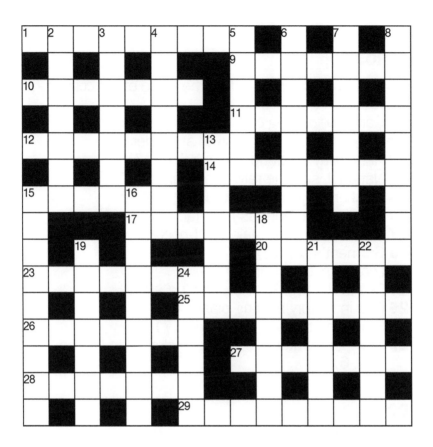

22 Born sound as a bell but in want (7)

24 Youngsters in strict training caught arranging dates (6)

48

ACROSS

1 Post-impressionists affect the value of his collection (11)
9 Gangster placing cowl in front of chimney (7)
10 Song of loyalty from worker at border (6)
12 Hand may crack up in coal-mine? (7)
13 National, say, the rate of exchange? (7)
14 Mockery of youth-leader joining club (5)
15 Small restaurant has front facing lake (9)
17 Marble, the most plain, is of poorest quality (9)
20 Garment's cuff (5)
22 Lock with loose spring? (7)
24 See in the physician concerning air (7)
25 One in factory making plastic (6)
26 Stand in Uttoxeter racecourse (7)
27 New perpetrator of off-the-peg clothes in France (4-1-6)

DOWN

2 Break for girl in religious setting (7)
3 Liable to go round with German – that can be checked! (9)
4 Food and drink to someone (5)
5 Post requiring literary knowledge (7)
6 One producing beads for a knitted garment (7)
7 They who take stock-from Phil's forest? (11)
8 Spud finds big sum at job-centre (6)
11 Containers taken from secret place (11)
16 One shows how high a Viscount is (9)
18 Western fisherman and fiddler (7)
19 Rave about high priest having faith (7)
20 Typical orientals, showing little heat (7)
21 Test of gold and lead, possibly (6)
23 Add measure of drink during flight (3,2)

49

ACROSS

1 A sign to spies about ancient language (7)
5 Is this bun otherwise included in tea? (7)
9 Lived at last on ridge? (5)
10 Strike a light? A stripper! (4-5)
11 Having lost one, Seles learnt to become merciless (10)
12 Expert on Queen (4)
14 Frenchman may do a brave translation of this novel? (6,6)
18 Shakily opposes ball at start of match that will eventually be fruitful (5-7)
21 Current I'd used in a battery (4)
22 Walks and tires out relative (10)
25 Large landmass classified as temperate (9)
26 Angry buccaneer losing his head (5)
27 Judge recapitulating in case – most uninteresting (7)
28 eg Ball I chopped on to this? (3,4)

DOWN

1 Totters, when bitten by them? (6)
2 One, say, brought up to 'andle antique (3-3)
3 Sounds like you ate, consumed by care, yet got thin (10)
4 Sailor in state of intrigue (5)
5 Where one of chapter lingers about middle of monastery? (9)
6 Lets out young sows (4)
7 Needs father in raising one of these sea mammals (8)
8 Is it a bit of a fag to empty them? (8)
13 Stop one to celebrate settling down (10)

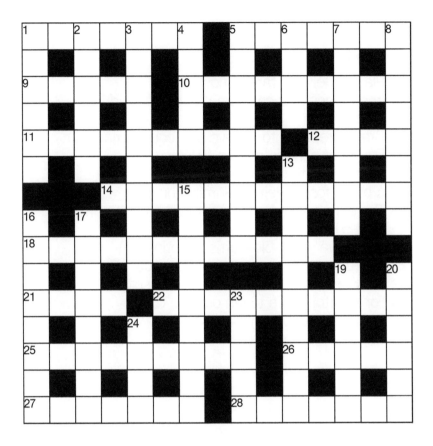

15 A large amount intended, we hear, for a share-out (9)

16 Even out lace band (8)

17 Stone's accepted into movie by choice (8)

19 Odd start to A-level (6)

20 Trial by fire or wood (6)

23 You'll find it in ring surrounding top of tulip! (5)

24 It's *not* found going back in the Med I think! (4)

50

ACROSS

1 Plain order, but fare almost rich (5)
4 Impudence and criticism makes one red in the face (8)
8 Grave prepared to receive sick countryman (8)
9 Frame of mind is a pose (8)
11 Confidently tipping off guard (7)
13 A place for bargains? Humiliation (9)
15 There's no support for mounting this bit of magic (6,4-5)
18 Reflective youth blossoms in spring (9)
21 Accounts that have everyone in knots (7)
22 They're toasted, but end up in the soup (8)
24 For a tortoise, it's tough outside (8)
25 Body and head of horse (8)
26 Say, want a pound (5)

DOWN

1 Share people's prediction (10)
2 Went back to pass in the road (8)
3 Personal attraction to unusual archaism (8)
4 In Istanbul, I raised this money (4)
5 A way to get frequent hassle (6)
6 Pay protection money? (6)
7 Bird that flies on end of string (4)
10 One ordered to keep silent (8)
12 Troops stuck in town, so raring for a scrap (8)
14 Assume formal hearing's cancelled (4,2,4)
16 In moving cab, I talk of traffic queue (8)
17 Incited a rebellious show (8)
19 Raw recruit that's sent to castle (6)
20 Interest on deed not touched (6)
22 Smart bird Ken left (4)
23 Hamish, for example, put son to bed (4)

51

ACROSS

1 Compulsory grounding for an aviator (6,7)
10 Clamp down on work force (7)
11 Available to discuss outside (4-3)
12 Place where economy of truth is fashionable (4)
13 Skip a beat and reduce (5)
14 Jar for a kind of berry (4)
17 The Magi seem upset in victory (4,3)
18 Sphere of vision (7)
19 Journey on such a train can only have one end (3-4)
22 Comfortable seat for a Turk (7)
24 Put a point to teetotaller engineer (4)
25 Checks part of the rigging (5)
26 It's drunk in the East Indies (4)
29 Eastern city doctor, now rich (7)
30 Violet's in unusually poor condition (7)
31 The Celtic girl out to provide illumination (8,5)

DOWN

2 He pours out music from his lyre in Greek mythology (7)
3 Student caught with a dictionary (2-2)
4 Rubbish collector (7)
5 Porter is about to dispatch messenger (7)
6 Expected to end in mortal combat (4)
7 A river once more rises and falls (7)
8 A blow in the back (9,4)
9 Device that should catch on, if handled properly (9,4)
15 Commonest name for a forger (5)
16 A mouthful of water (5)
20 Old city in part of South Africa is unaffected (7)
21 American sportsman in jug? (7)

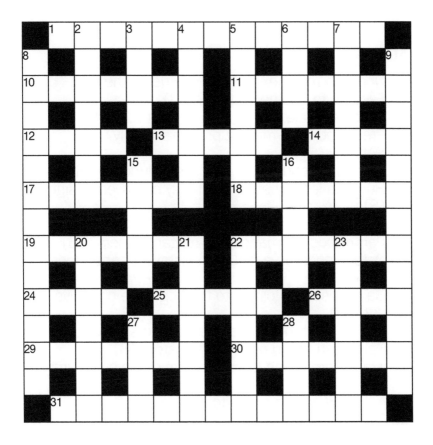

22 Imply small company is involved in games, perhaps (7)

23 Oratorio is a new production in the network (7)

27 Revolutionary entertainment (4)

28 Baked beans need this lid for protection (4)

52

ACROSS

1 One with much experience boards on the right (6)
4 Face up to another drink (3,2,3)
8 Extremely pale, having spent about £2 (6)
9 Prevented from making progress mainly? (8)
10 Setting? (8)
11 Certain second person in Paris included a stitch (6)
12 Hundred less locating one fancy engraved design (8)
13 Reg's so upset the big lady (6)
15 Part of body demanded by militant miners? (6)
18 Deterioration as a result of mistake by attendant (8)
20 Gains respect, going into the bog while on active duty (6)
21 Rubbing out the fifth and sixth letters opposite (8)
23 Spicy dish found on top of the stove (8)
24 Island comprising three-quarters of the old country (6)
25 A getting back again after illness (8)
26 Simply like one in the city (6)

DOWN

1 It is splendid to have a drink with the queen (5)
2 Abnormal growth on one insect that stings lizard (9)
3 Colourful mound near the M25 (7)
4 Theatre-goers don't need to travel to get it (6,2,7)
5 Artist modelling aspic as well (7)
6 Wrong waterway causes anguish (7)
7 One named in the post (9)
12 Very agitated whilst having a wash? (2,1,6)
14 Blame Bill with debts who is grasping (9)
16 Ape-like? (7)
17 Not having a score, but more than twelve (7)

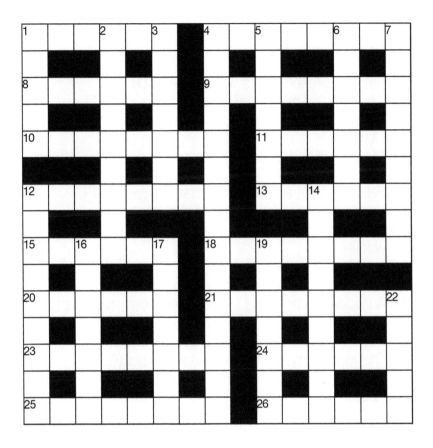

19 Effective batting strength? (2,5)
22 Rough blast you initially concluded (5)

53

ACROSS

1 Lasting present – it's well-made (10)
9 Churlish, as are many in the French way (4)
10 A right little renegade, or so the referee appears (10)
11 Make a stand and one's accommodated by others (6)
12 Fellow taking a phone-call that's a real trial (7)
15 Blow up in the home – start exploding! (7)
16 Great get-together of fighting man and social worker (5)
17 Incline to run wild (4)
18 To struggle without money is awful (4)
19 A goddess demands some reverence – respect (5)
21 The craftsman trains a replacement (7)
22 Petition about the hunt (7)
24 The leaning type often showing stress (6)
27 Those making plans for the Arctic's development (10)
28 Gather to see a popular friar (4)
29 Points dividing a mathematician and film director (10)

DOWN

2 He wants listening equipment left behind (4)
3 Thrill, though only a bit (6)
4 A portion of food fulfilling requirements (7)
5 Little creatures making efforts because dropped (4)
6 A massive rock split a great stream (7)
7 Thinking to show spirit, invite a rebel (10)
8 A community resolution (10)
12 They offer simple remedies (10)
13 Letting in or letting on (10)
14 Handed over certain information about a quartet (5)

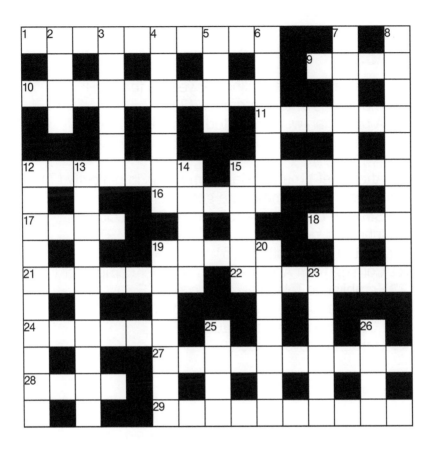

15 Conclude this could be made finer (5)
19 A drop of water (7)
20 Cut and dry and turn it over (7)
23 Run around with lawless set causing anxiety (6)
25 Galatea's beloved. Bill is all for him (4)
26 A case of pins and needles (4)

54

ACROSS

1 Musical talent a stallholder yearns for (7,5)
8 Many girls in tuition groups (7)
9 A physician was promoted by saintly bishop (7)
11 Journalist taken aback by malice, notwithstanding (7)
12 After brief time Russian currency is in difficulty (7)
13 Forced to accommodate good woman (5)
14 Strange dream once related by Boccaccio (9)
16 Inherited by constituents of Lancaster (9)
19 Should need nothing (5)
21 Coming from Arkansas with another competitor (7)
23 Established fête likely to succeed (3,4)
24 Guardian spirits made son reform (7)
25 I translated a Latin language (7)
26 Liars with novel ideas (12)

DOWN

1 Party leader uplifted when paid tribute (7)
2 After relaxation I have become uneasy (7)
3 English capitalist finds purpose in Church festival (4,5)
4 Quality paintings are shown up by it (5)
5 Bearing flowers for stylish British weaver (2,5)
6 Batter one's belongings (7)
7 College gains a minor acting trophy (7,5)
10 Lover's gift to atone for all-time ding-dong? (8,4)
15 Church design Stella and I regarded as heavenly (9)
17 Present-day electricity charge (7)
18 Various changes wrought by the Messiah? (7)
19 Silver in bizarre setting causes grave offence (7)
20 Sauces I discovered in tombs (7)
22 Inclination expressed by composer (5)

55

ACROSS

7 Take out a line – time can be allowed (9)
8 Polish woman requiring quarters (5)
10 Almost score, but not quite (8)
11 Men did badly, and that's resented (6)
12 A port some sailors dread entering (4)
13 Tries to lure into a back-street (8)
15 Greek maid serving a celebration meal (7)
17 Lacking common sense – a shortcoming in the egghead (7)
20 She certainly created a row! (8)
22 A means to get off (4)
25 Like a little company after retiring if a failure (6)
26 Points to wrong-doers sanction (8)
27 A store of French cannabis (5)
28 Those who consider life barely worth living (9)

DOWN

1 A talent for making money in the market (5)
2 Threaten a naughty child with some result (6)
3 A girl tuned in before they could investigate (8)
4 The schoolboy ain't one to change! (7)
5 Feature about style for country people (8)
6 Once more showing the traveller as a consumer (9)
9 Discharge date is coming up (4)
14 Hangers-on traipse, as played out (9)
16 A type causing hostility (8)
18 Attract attention, being a good man and striking (5,3)
19 Top man putting points in regal fashion (7)
21 An element that's in the air one breathes (4)
23 Notes assault is fearful (6)
24 Make a start, though it's a struggle (3-2)

56

ACROSS

1 Music comes from this plumbing behind the basin (3-5)

9 No government supporter makes such stirring speeches (8)

10 Family saving money for oven (4)

11 Fair sample of angry group (5,7)

13 Goaded donkey raced around (8)

15 Cast off (6)

16 Provide strong conclusion (4)

17 Note return of sun: sign to take something off (5)

18 Partially-collapsed area of church (4)

20 Flower book for Christmas, perhaps (6)

21 Suffering after-effects of poor catering? (8)

23 Determination shown by protected tenant? (7,5)

26 Team of one? (4)

27 Italian motorway and country roads heading east (8)

28 Girl locked up, having been extravagant (8)

DOWN

2 Estrange with a fib – neat construction (8)

3 Married couple worked hand-in-glove to amuse the kids (5,3,4)

4 Dialect peculiar to Pisa (6)

5 Announces 22 on board (4)

6 Classic age, not so great (8)

7 Some home tuition for housewife (4)

8 It's not fair describing her colouring (8)

12 A call for judgment, with this winning card to play? (3,4,5)

14 Teacher or patron (5)

16 For me, sea when rough is terrifying (8)

17 Am over to stay, but pretend to be ill (8)

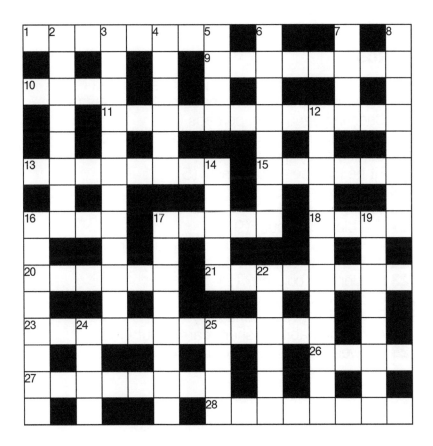

19 Authorise penalty (8)
22 Invariably, Irish county's short of a leader (6)
24 Colleague means everything to you at first (4)
25 See me work up an ode, say (4)

57

ACROSS

1 Beg to start with bread and cheese spread (7)
5 Monday's arrangement for current suppliers (7)
9 Cheering eggs it on, perhaps (7)
10 Grain that is developed in African republic (7)
11 Carries away the gates (9)
12 Fit he may be – at a pinch! (5)
13 Shoots game (5)
15 VV? (4-1-4)
17 The bloom of youth (9)
19 He tangles with cop—that will mean time (5)
22 Won a hand and won the game (5)
23 Leader of a column? (9)
25 Cutting and running (7)
26 R Mugabe gives offence (7)
27 A training habit we shed tears about (7)
28 Involves mending the net before setting sail (7)

DOWN

1 One-sided support for literature (4-3)
2 Course for beginners (7)
3 Tea break about six for Mrs Peron (5)
4 Puts restriction on movement and worker strikes (9)
5 Has a meal in readiness (5)
6 Arrange a loan and I get a note in exchange (9)
7 Swallow one cocktail (7)
8 Take it from the horse's mouth (7)
14 Nips back to float in the spray (9)
16 I've sub-let converted entrance hall (9)
17 Retribution seems in order (7)
18 Deserter's retreat (3-4)
20 Employment of paper folders (7)
21 They have titles within their grasp (7)
23 Enigmatic composer (5)
24 Put gold coin into circulation (5)

58

ACROSS

1 Three ways to make progress in sport (3,4,3,4)
9 Discovered appearance of the French who had not been spoken well of (8)
10 Temptress's warning? (5)
12 Man, a bit of a thug, has appeared (4)
13 Unromantic lover? (10)
15 One who favours cooking of his own kind (8)
16 Cutter, namely, they manoeuvred (6)
18 Went first as well going round for a sword (6)
20 Company placed before you and me repeatedly a North African dish (8)
23 Short dance arrangement seems likely (2,3,5)
24 Staunch supporter of a flower (4)
26 Sounded like a nosy person, one in order (5)
27 Break one's nose (8)
28 Be good at distinguishing vegetables? (4,4,6)

DOWN

2 Old man Ronald accepts silver model (7)
3 Antelope kicked up dust underneath initially (4)
4 Odd individual (8)
5 Knotty problem being without medicine? (6)
6 Lest it has very recently been packed (4,2,4)
7 Left-winger, one right then wrong in the fog (7)
8 Also after that time a few, plenty more than that (3,4,4)
11 Soldiers one could be offended by? (5-6)
14 Moderately intellectual in second line below the centre (10)
17 Courage of a type on the cape (8)
19 Transfer Hal into Edinburgh area (7)
21 Continually active whilst in decline? (2,3,2)
22 Copy of the same type (6)
25 Man constantly featured (4)

59

ACROSS

1 One who's barely prepared for a quick move (8)
5 Liveliness as a result of drink? (6)
9 Went when put right (8)
10 The doctor too may be a cowboy! (6)
12 Grind can appear repulsive (9)
13 Bag a prize (5)
14 Waste wood (4)
16 People retain a right to travel – battle for it (7)
19 Withdraw hurt (7)
21 Underworld boss taking large number round flat (4)
24 The show went on mid-October (5)
25 Blue – Conservative – that's plain (9)
27 Has a meal during the flight? (4,2)
28 Green grain, not for cooking (8)
29 Quarter a Parisian with the German or separate (6)
30 Gloomy character turning poet against the head (8)

DOWN

1 Chopped capers to make a pickle (6)
2 Wave to show anger about double-parking (6)
3 Name for a girl – Celia possibly (5)
4 With little hesitation put out English recluse (7)
6 Drips toiling? (9)
7 Torn about invariably being deferential (8)
8 Started working when attacked (6,2)
11 Name some better man (4)
15 Courted in order to propose (9)
17 They wrongly assume money-lenders carry small change (8)
18 Market town with continuous charge arrangement (8)
20 Leather shroud (4)
21 Elderly lady in complete flutter (7)

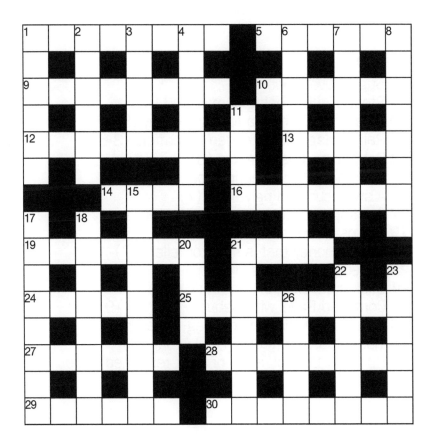

22 Brown got up in time, so it's related (6)
23 Craft keeps a picture collection in the USA (6)
26 Writing a letter for a Greek, the medico gets a diamond (5)

60

ACROSS

1 Suggestive mood (10)
6 State of a hut being demolished (4)
10 A name in California for a waterway (5)
11 Rail carriage not intended for puffers (3-6)
12 Pot and tin basin broken (8)
13 Watered garden wearing socks, say (5)
15 A sty is such an ugly thing (7)
17 Starting to develop northern climb (7)
19 Learns a trick for magazine (7)
21 Ready money that is right for teller? (7)
22 Racecourse records order (5)
24 Cock a snook in cotton fabric (8)
27 Confused Ravel with Debussy opening (9)
28 A stroke touching middle peg is clever (5)
29 Instructed, reportedly, in civil wrong (4)
30 Harvey & Co took a cut of what remained to be divided (10)

DOWN

1 Small island of some chinchillas (4)
2 New gear among sandhills is working gear (9)
3 Stop in Panama (5)
4 Defendable, with most of team fit? (7)
5 Meat cooked in ovens (7)
7 Delights in Keats, possibly (5)
8 In this place, letter slipped into engagement-book can be passed on (10)
9 English parliamentarian has one son in stress (8)
14 Fed up with a binder that shows signs of vandalism (10)
16 Hide unguent (8)
18 Latest addresses in Cambridge, for example? (9)
20 Get nothing back on a litre of wool-dressing (7)

21 WWII commando's language, caught outside (7)
23 Indian instrument is troubled by pitch (5)
25 Host was unusually jolly (5)
26 Coins buried in Treasure Island (4)

61

ACROSS

1 Travel authority gives vehicle approval (3,4)
5 Eyeshield protecting Italian guest (7)
9 Breaking up can be very painful (9)
10 Hanging is a bit of an embarrassment (5)
11 Make money abroad as a senior (5)
12 Win over, with circular argument? (4,5)
13 Feeling excitement (9)
16 Southern fir needs trunk support (5)
17 Work to break strike? Buzz off! (3,2)
18 Release a chap who's beholden to none (4,5)
20 A super Tom is prepared – to kill Jerry? (9)
23 Please donate a rib (5)
25 Animal whose horn I found terrible (5)
26 Let off bill, left (9)
27 Foolish ritual, turning Eastern monarch into embalmed body (7)
28 Prematurely go round extremes of Greece with extreme enthusiasm (7)

DOWN

1 Good queen eats fish, too (7)
2 Odds to fix in spread (5)
3 Be present with soldier as escort (9)
4 Did he write rapidly? (5)
5 Invite lag to become security guard (9)
6 The way appearance gives you a bit of a lift (5)
7 Greenish and quite sour, alas (9)
8 What's left to regret about beaten side (7)
14 The sea-god in his element here? (9)
15 Deduce, we hear, girl is in hospital (9)
16 Closely following performance, including commercial (9)
17 Sing wordlessly to instrument – boring (7)

19 Duet, say, to perform today in America (7)
21 Awaken girl – all right to go in (5)
22 We hear it's the height of irritation (5)
24 Bury in hinterland (5)

62

ACROSS

1 Keeper takes dog beside a hill (7)
5 Group conceals gear from robber (7)
9 A Frenchman pocketing classy ointment (7)
10 By dint of a street diversion, end up far away (7)
11 Vulgar squad makes vigorous onslaught (9)
12 Right, everyone! Stretch! (5)
13 It's used by plastics producer to keep son in check (5)
15 Sadly, nice pets died on being examined (9)
17 Fellow worker makes army officer join association (9)
19 Get smaller lighter (5)
22 Stress an addict usually concealed (5)
23 Communicate successfully to buy a crucifix (3,6)
25 False evidence by adjudicating panel (7)
26 Eton was refurbished without difficulty (2,5)
27 Initially really jubilant, as reported (7)
28 Husband has to join the forces again (7)

DOWN

1 Nightspot habitué guilty of armed assault? (7)
2 Ogres in destructive assault on large areas (7)
3 Material of current worth in Scotland (5)
4 A shopkeeper's job involves passing on gossip (9)
5 Ordered to retain key symbol (5)
6 Rebellious gunners run amok in it (9)
7 A formic queen is quite immovable (7)
8 Many were irritated by being abandoned (7)
14 Wants new wine: It's the only option (5,4)
16 Incentive to use a sugar substitute (9)
17 The cutter is a sailing-boat (7)
18 Subsequently got a quid on the side (7)
20 A number held up by noble explorer (7)

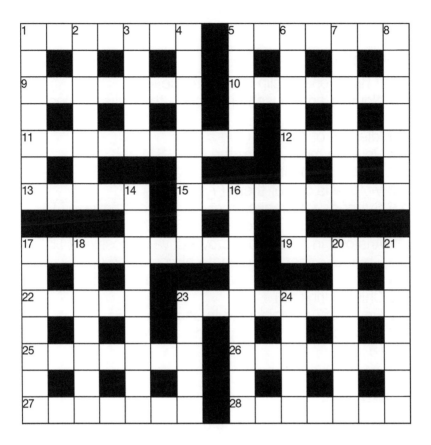

21 Test ore afresh to gain award (7)
23 Ridiculed fellow with education (5)
24 Lots of performers have squints (5)

63

ACROSS

8 It helps one to slip into a brogue (8)

9 Not just an amusement arcade that fails to open (6)

10 Idle talk of rent-cut (3)

11 Relation moving from the east (8)

12 Cautious about one foot being slippery (6)

13 Victoria is one of them (7,8)

15 Supports for breaks, involving end of traction (7)

18 Trained doctor carries sick-notes (7)

21 Aristotle in fuss about provocative disposition (15)

24 State of mineral aggregate almost used up (6)

25 Late in the day for slack water, you say? (8)

26 Child's drink (3)

27 Figure of university held in ceremony (6)

28 Aquatic mammal, in spread hay, moved unsteadily (8)

DOWN

1 Nervous condition of one of the Tiger economies, we hear (6)

2 Happened to live on hill (6)

3 His work has a human aspect (8,7)

4 Being British, she takes gin with the student (7)

5 Does it finally take a turn for the better? (7,8)

6 On holiday here in France, a new driver is licensed (8)

7 I stand corrected at church for absence (8)

14 Unlucky in early part of millennium (3)

16 Look up in equality? That is a contradiction! (8)

17 Angry about equipment to water fields (8)

19 Some believe fiction (3)

20 Capital investment for a father? (7)

22 Underworld name and number (6)

23 Ends do need changing when waterlogged (6)

64

ACROSS

1 Business to get involved in by force (10)
6 Fine powder available in metal canisters (4)
10 With the sovereign due, created a beastly row (5)
11 French family-man accepting break to keep going (9)
12 Mark urban area's poverty (8)
13 Instruct a class (5)
15 Dress hire cut by intention (7)
17 Hibernating insects without number (7)
19 Beaten, and that's material (7)
21 An artist's jacket (7)
22 The odd scholar makes music (5)
24 Spent recklessly – laid on about six (8)
27 Track supervision (9)
28 City miser's re-housed (5)
29 A high-flier has merit, we hear (4)
30 The sea mole (10)

DOWN

1 Look up about fifty elusive people (4)
2 The outside broadcast is his forte (9)
3 Equestrian appendage (5)
4 Corded stuff isn't commonly put on a new coat (7)
5 A high-minded person, ready for a change, transgressed (7)
7 Correct guys in publicity (5)
8 Net account for providing church lighting (10)
9 Concerned with track access (8)
14 Keep access! (10)
16 Going in for charm (8)
18 Ancient scientist claims the compound made (9)
20 The doctor includes everyone that's idler (7)
21 Plain van, as an organisation required (7)

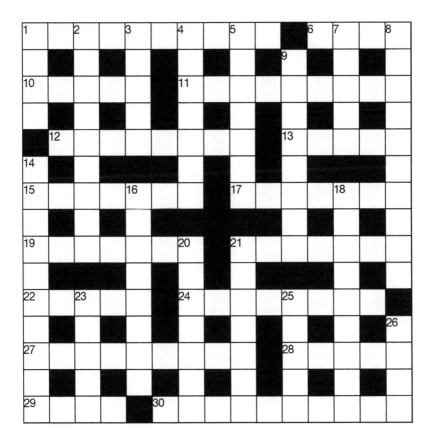

23 A Scotsman carrying gold – the fool! (5)
25 Payment commonly secured by a twister (5)
26 Old ruler seen in his finest sarong (4)

65

ACROSS

1 Money not permanently invested in *HMS Belfast*? (8,7)
9 Vibration vibrating on a screen (9)
10 Lost in transit perhaps (2,3)
11 Tune Leo composed about solvent (7)
12 Artillerymen follow hectic competitive activity (3,4)
13 It cannot fly in Australia (3)
14 Quickly get to a point near the M6 (7)
17 Harbour one commanding officer by the colonnade (7)
19 Open race I had shortly entered (7)
22 Wager about one with Ronald getting a title (7)
24 Do something with letters as announced (3)
25 More distant meteor spinning right at the start (7)
26 Cocktail required, a cider's ordered (7)
28 It's unacceptable either way (3,2)
29 Copy not left of restriction (9)
30 What correspondents need to do with anagrams (8,7)

DOWN

1 What many said to be deceptive start by actor (5,10)
2 Blackbird left river first (5)
3 Touch-line (7)
4 Material woven by Anne and Ken (7)
5 Tidy way to solve a mystery (5,2)
6 David's works in book form (7)
7 The devil of an Australian islander? (9)
8 Make tracks so others can follow (5,10)
15 I get manic, terribly, when's it's puzzling (9)
16 Have topless dress (3)
18 Love Virginia has of eggs (3)

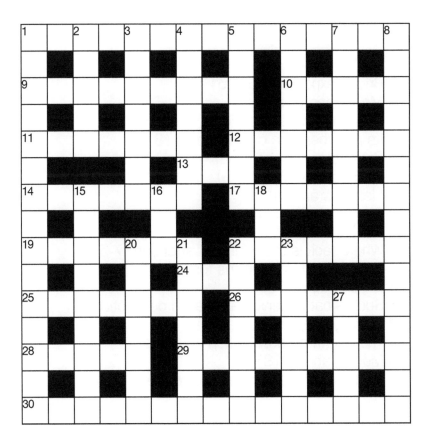

20 Land moved into sea (7)
21 Going round the corner (7)
22 Despite being brutish, bales it out (7)
23 Penny once in Tirana could have been beaming with joy (7)
27 Agree to strike (5)

66

ACROSS

1 Bridge expert in court (6)
4 Moved camp (8)
9 Lapped and beaten (6)
10 Its members are outnumbered (8)
12 Grass blown in the wind? (4)
13 We hear it is healthy (5)
14 I left to start work (4)
17 Record playing in the small hours – mood indigo? (12)
20 Where Jack is the centre of attention (7-5)
23 Former graduate returns for a test (4)
24 Lift shafts, we hear (5)
25 Such a cat deserves a detailed description (4)
28 Movingly depict an academic (8)
29 The length an association will go to? (6)
30 Moving about? (8)
31 Wrongly admits to be at the centre of things (6)

DOWN

1 Badly garbled direction to raise capital (8)
2 Swell position for a batsman (8)
3 They're down to play bingo (4)
5 Rows among allies end in cordiality (12)
6 Archbishop of York has to dress up (4)
7 Man of the cloth has a follower, we hear (6)
8 This helps fishermen bring the catch to the surface (3-3)
11 Discussion with a specialist about coolant units (12)
15 It moves the helicopter, up or down (5)
16 It has wings and flies (5)
18 Upset caused by greed and corruption (8)
19 Clumsy former spouse in Pinter play (8)

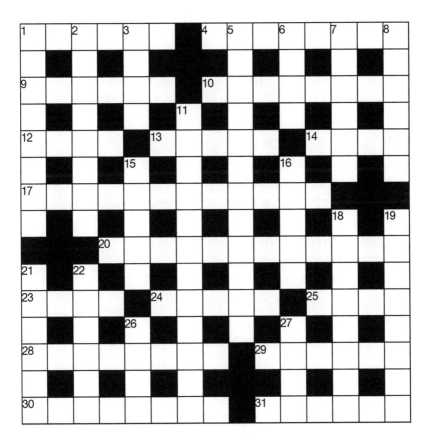

21 It never rains but it pours (6)
22 Transport for student with a university final (6)
26 In certain charts it may indicate a mile (4)
27 Side of fresh meat (4)

67

ACROSS

1 Staggering away from the scales (3,7)
6 A service return from a long way back (4)
9 Miser takes economical fish (10)
10 Four points made in bulletin (4)
12 Slowly moved – only part of foot each time? (6)
13 It takes the strain in the kitchen (8)
15 Repeatedly with a profit after period (4,3,5)
18 How inn traded badly – complete waste (4,3,5)
21 Old exam concerning rural life (8)
22 Infer energy's used in car journey (6)
24 Goddess appears one's double (4)
25 Sticky worker given notice? (4-6)
26 Near dark – not quite (4)
27 Temp ranted about organisation of office (10)

DOWN

1 Porch ideal to display bloom (6)
2 Violent fire destroyed church (6)
3 Just estimation of the added value (12)
4 Egyptian cross Khan was injured (4)
5 Skimp on work, but reduce dangerous moments (3,7)
7 Army exercise deadly if done wrong (5,3)
8 After holiday, call to repair racquet (8)
11 Fall for Milton's work (8,4)
14 The very number for such a team game! (5-1-4)
16 Notice the choice for approval (8)
17 Distorting, wicked wit may hurt (8)
19 Move quietly to East after advice (6)
20 Search out bishop in parts of the yard (6)
23 Request for parking on field (4)

68

ACROSS

1 Australian miner (6)
4 To dance with Dorothy has become a regular pattern (5,3)
8 Ridiculed after being promoted (4,2)
9 Cardinal distinction (8)
10 Vile Rose somehow remains on top (8)
11 Only an ass wants orange squash (6)
12 It makes a modest punter excited (8)
13 Account about one sovereign raising tax in France (6)
15 Humour a procurer (6)
18 Tries to incorporate everything in the casserole, maybe (8)
20 Coming for the pre-Christmas period (6)
21 No longer on the stage – it's very hard (8)
23 Only about one NCO? That's an absurdity! (8)
24 Blame admitted by the German retailer (6)
25 What a pity! That's twice as costly (4,4)
26 Initially no ensign ever did every duty as required (6)

DOWN

1 It plays the new CDs I love (5)
2 Socialise and buy a lot of drinks (3,6)
3 Agent is not to change the decoration (7)
4 Gave order to release upstream vessel (8,7)
5 Felled a hooligan without help (4,3)
6 Professor blown by high wind in Ireland? (7)
7 Obsequious people cause feeling of revulsion (3,6)
12 A copper cracked up on being assessed (9)
14 I shall take a card, however discomfited (3,2,4)
16 Month Fitzgerald published a short story (7)
17 Dilapidated latrine on a sailing-ship (7)

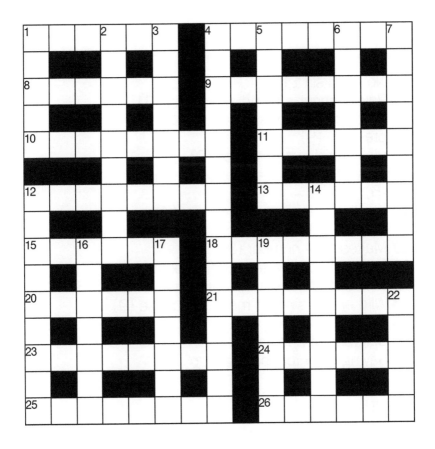

19 The Devil is a wicked fellow (7)
22 Died after blood shed at the corrida? (5)

69

ACROSS

1 No thanks! (11)
10 Pale, without a friend, took cover (3)
11 Mischievous type starts a law suit under great pressure (9)
12 Pink vehicle used to race (9)
13 Type of column made of some solid or icy material (5)
14 Leave quietly – good gracious! (4)
15 Assiduous boss had debts (8)
17 Makes up a number (8)
19 Mother had an afterthought about the plans (4)
22 Some of Arthur's trunks are made of wood (5)
23 Wild animals might make less noise (9)
25 Tense and below par (9)
26 Disgrace of a fool (3)
27 Saying sorry for spoiling a go (11)

DOWN

2 The lowest point of a messy drain (5)
3 Agent scoffs, but goes over it again (7)
4 Rita managed to include four things which were not at all important (6)
5 Hair pieces can cause the greatest problems (8)
6 Determined policemen went into action (7)
7 Way to get rid of the professor of physics, perhaps? (8,5)
8 Visitor left, throwing out caustic criticisms (8)
9 Easily excel at removing blemishes (5,5,3)
14 Lets stick fall to get sweets (8)
16 Just fancy spring water (4,4)
18 Rocky place for hardy plants perhaps (7)
20 Perpetually young animal carries oriental member back (7)

21 Susan's surname often has a novel appearance? (6)

24 You're not the first to get a wooden one! (5)

70

ACROSS

1 Detailed list few find flexible (7)
5 A journalist saying this can be cutting (7)
9 Fancy putting a hundred on a charge! (7)
10 The drawbacks of writing about popular practice (7)
11 Frown and moon around in future (4,3,2)
12 The board expected to answer by letter (5)
13 A bird seen about late in the day (5)
15 The Italian left with a gibe when disturbed (3,2,4)
17 Judges a rider's about to crack up (9)
19 Keep back bread for distribution (5)
22 A bouquet? There's a romantic beginning! (5)
23 Quiet serving men shaving and grooming (9)
25 Striking seal – it's huge (7)
26 Superior wear? (7)
27 Skip Oriental gin (7)
28 Coach transport provided with a certain hesitation (7)

DOWN

1 A match for the devil (7)
2 Have a meal, then sit and think (7)
3 The hunter will go on about port! (5)
4 A little white flower highly regarded in Europe (9)
5 Sound article for me (5)
6 Red cotton all in knots (9)
7 Verses among the tersest in an anthology (7)
8 Carry on about a way loss is being made (7)
14 Turning a name into an issue (9)
16 The boor interrupted by a woman's attacks (6,3)
17 Perplexed, as a lot's not right (2,1,4)
18 A person planning to spend time idly – about fifty (7)
20 The thinker holds it to be a great country (7)

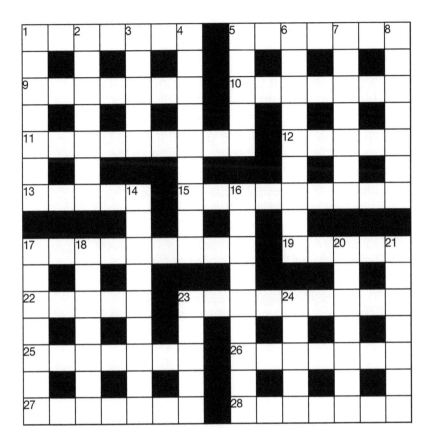

21 Orderly having to pull up and back around (7)
23 A portion of convenience food taken to church (5)
24 The scene of conflict near a roundabout (5)

71

ACROSS

1 Plenty to eat, but won't it go round? (6,4)
6 This could be the reason why I didn't walk out (4)
10 Return of drink in the marketplace (5)
11 Complaint that could be painful to face (9)
12 One drunkard or another returning to the place (7)
13 They go off to the match (7)
14 Such an act needs forethought (12)
18 Sign language first in the books (12)
21 Bowler to employ too many (7)
23 Gangster Robin left with word of hesitation (7)
24 Disturbed our Cretan storyteller (9)
25 Terrorists gave us the slip (5)
26 An impossible date in Ireland (4)
27 Secret place not starting to be designed for container (10)

DOWN

1 Protection, say, going round iron model (6)
2 One French male and all the others creating a disturbance (6)
3 Westminster steak-house? (4,10)
4 Dwarf missile (9)
5 A daintily pleasing accent (5)
7 Target, ie fluttering bird (8)
8 Car port! (8)
9 Second celebrity? (3,2,3,6)
15 *Black Beauty?* (4,5)
16 From IOM, Edgar used symbol to represent a word (8)
17 Shrill and harsh like an owl? (8)
19 Magic Circle minister (6)
20 Part held by schemer generally to come into view (6)
22 Point taken by nice relative (5)

72

ACROSS

1 Fool, to accept passenger (4,3,1,4)
9 Discussion group remains perplexed (7)
10 Observed dirt on floor of old pub (7)
11 Gorilla, say, to cross peak (4)
12 Contract for boxer's fee (5)
13 A little slug likes fruit (4)
16 Trellis the French put round loft (7)
17 Poor respect for symbol of authority (7)
18 Sharp-eyed old boy missed attendant (7)
21 Vessel – one going up and down on waves? (7)
23 Principal said to have long hair (4)
24 Strong chance of search for weapons (5)
25 I can trouble old American (4)
28 Out of the running, but won back woman with energy (7)
29 For Cockney, to have anger is normal (7)
30 Treatment that goes swimmingly? (12)

DOWN

1 Encountered rising annoyance in storm (7)
2 Helpful sort (4)
3 A lot of money for a strain (7)
4 Objects to holidays one's accepted (7)
5 Lines taken in arguments (4)
6 Ecstasy, say, with which to receive fabric (7)
7 Let his best man come from the regular staff (13)
8 Knock cask, getting scab (6-7)
14 Bird, an enormous creature (5)
15 King takes in romantic poet (5)
19 Ladder from home used by escaper (7)
20 Peak income perhaps in the fast stream (7)
21 Spend a long time in corridor (7)
22 Needing food, going round a country (7)

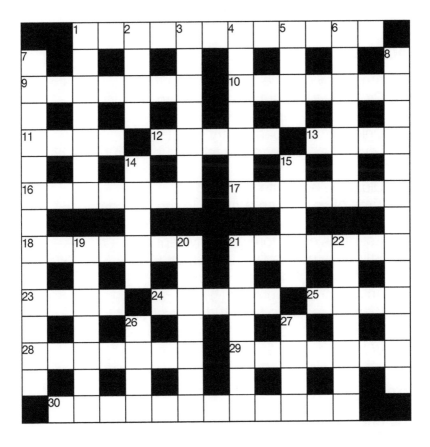

26 Raise the back (4)
27 Big game shot (4)

73

ACROSS

1 Arrived by chance at Arthur's court (7)
5 Crowd is turbulent, showing alarm (7)
9 Regretting I kept in step (5)
10 Onlooker sees bad sentry shot (9)
11 Love wife – observe the technique to embrace her (10)
12 Old lady, not quite dignified (4)
14 Time of year when a guy is in the hot seat (7,5)
18 Urge caustic piece in paper to be removed (5,7)
21 Count as one's foreign equivalent (4)
22 Still have position with a railway (10)
25 Stunt paid off for arguer (9)
26 Animal ridden from hill (5)
27 Warrant received from rude server (7)
28 Tacky worker, say, more depressed about money (7)

DOWN

1 Bright colour gives church a lift (6)
2 People accept help from girl (6)
3 Flashy building to steer clear of? (10)
4 Lie around black board (5)
5 Run away twice? Not this soldier (6,3)
6 Quiet – notice fish (4)
7 Lacking a majority (5,3)
8 People entitled to see one in hospital (8)
13 Not told loveless union created (10)
15 Eccentric person in Genoa (9)
16 Use stored money – I'd find that grand (8)
17 Mental problem of North European relative (8)
19 Instruction book not automatically available (6)
20 Funny story about first to eat mollusc (6)
23 Lugs to set up (5)
24 Litigant finds speaking a drain (4)

74

ACROSS

1 Brings up the subject of jewellery, by the sound of it (8)
5 Stoppage resulting from armed raid (4-2)
8 The cobbler's there – and not before time! (2,4)
9 Urge factory to serve vegetable (8)
10 Swindled – by the pet-shop proprietor? (4,1,3)
11 Stranded after a horse suffered injury (6)
12 Beam with heavy weight attached floating in the ocean (8)
13 Henry loves vigorous dance (4,2)
15 Offer to supply ship's dinghy (6)
18 Quietly tell boy off for having a beer-gut (3-5)
20 A crescendo is needed too (2,4)
21 Rang again after annulment was made (8)
23 I'm in on Dominican's first moves to gain control? (8)
24 Son interrupts famous hunter in prayer (6)
25 Having to make admission (6)
26 Anglican monarch introduced to Catholic storyteller (8)

DOWN

1 To make money one needs nerve (5)
2 Performed in a pop group and left (9)
3 Potential no-go area in the Tropics? (3,4)
4 Businessman who doesn't manage to find a mate (8,7)
5 Monopolise the laundry? Rubbish! (7)
6 Recall troops after lottery cancellation (4,3)
7 Clearly accommodating one with tolerance (9)
12 Finished by the demand for written proof of settlement! (3,4,2)
14 Finds method of working on speech about sport (9)

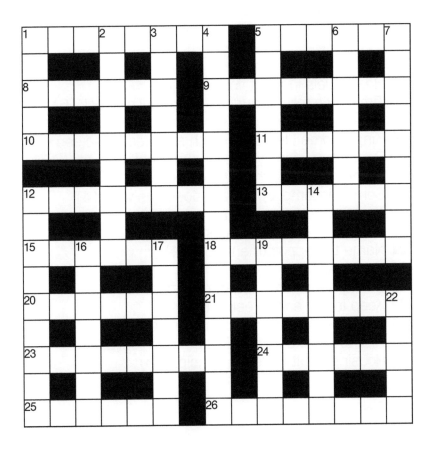

16 Point admitted by caring male reporter (7)
17 Loaded – with money and drink (7)
19 Local dance studio (7)
22 Rex and Enid returned from the restaurant (5)

75

ACROSS

1 Heavy fuels in great volume (8)
5 Timid little fellow caught by a surprise attack (6)
9 Dwelling is rented out (8)
10 King George I left the French a protective screen (6)
12 Deal allows deputy to hold about half of them (9)
13 Drunks receiving the right orders (5)
14 Some nincompoop usually does this work (4)
16 There's often a catch in it (7)
19 Regard cleanup as nonsense (3-4)
21 Name the appointment hour (4)
24 Hard-back (5)
25 Quietly considered an affront offered (9)
27 Keep it and earn breaks (6)
28 Periodical repository for ammunition (8)
29 First to be affected by Eastern conflict (6)
30 Housing adult males in principle (8)

DOWN

1 Wound on the head (6)
2 Put in this month without hesitation (6)
3 Sneakily move the team accepting money (5)
4 They cut things fine (7)
6 Constituents forget his prescience (9)
7 Reacting in rash fashion? (8)
8 Manoeuvres of rider and groom over time (8)
11 Mount before backing (4)
15 Dispute is on the level and he'll seek legal redress (9)
17 Poles involved in rescue making reproaches (8)
18 Watch a person who does it again (8)
20 A writer's confidence (4)
21 There's evidence of a leak – read the paper! (7)
22 A quarter possibly tried to walk (6)

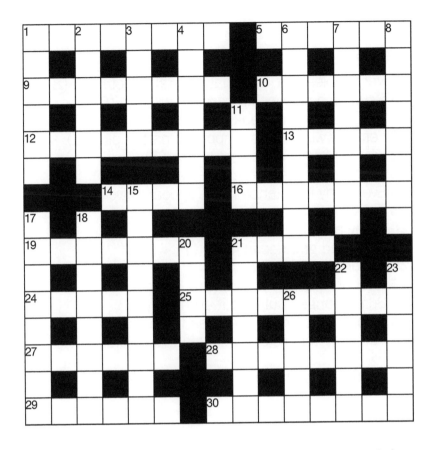

23 Five hundred will be in a hole before Christmas (6)
26 Cheer up retiring relation with a note (5)

76

ACROSS

1 Very unpleasant, and that's certainly not right! (8)
5 Scuttles a ship with a cargo of wildfowl (6)
9 Judge times tea break (8)
10 Left one with a most important part to play (6)
12 Like college-head, object to rise (6)
13 Giving carte blanche to the French rave (8)
15 Everybody in entertainment appears frivolous (7)
16 Tackle retreating soldiers for example (4)
20 Many a worker is not able (4)
21 Infuriated grandee in revolt (7)
25 Reports looked at (8)
26 After six the wise man shows his face (6)
28 Burn in anger, but sign it eventually (6)
29 Being by the water, liked sea to be rough (8)
30 Puff after middle-age – obtain this helpful device (6)
31 Upon this write after a vehicle number (8)

DOWN

1 Understand a proverb can divert youngsters (6)
2 No backward city, it gets a mention (6)
3 Woman modelling a man's hat (8)
4 Small creatures – some may be left standing (4)
6 Shut down before the end of August for the recess (6)
7 Passé but striking and not without admirers (8)
8 Shivers as the stars appear (8)
11 People who are late occupy his attention (7)
14 Lay clutching thin covering (7)
17 Carol carries little cash, which is discerning (8)
18 In consequence the cord gets twisted (8)
19 Forwarded about ten cents as a deposit (8)
22 Worm serving summons on a fellow (6)

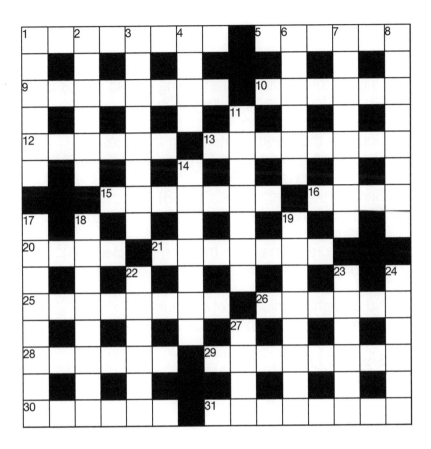

23 An Irishman in a film (6)
24 "Angels and ministers of grace —— us!"
Shakespeare's *Hamlet* (6)
27 Wall decoration means nothing to father (4)

77

ACROSS

1 Unlikely to get hitched, remaining unsold (4,2,3,5)
9 Gran is tipsy on a Spanish punch (7)
10 Case for the diplomat (7)
11 Some of the cheap seats are in the recess (4)
12 Creep with gun crazily holding an aversion (10)
14 Take the wrong way (6)
15 Spray article given to skinflint (8)
17 Novice putting one drink with new head into another! (8)
18 One's more clumsy with the atomic nucleus (6)
21 Report a group of conservationists or an office worker (10)
22 No draught in this part of the pub? (4)
24 Lot rely, strangely enough, on using this in a supermarket (7)
25 Snappy? (7)
26 Act like a fool? (4,10)

DOWN

1 Scenes leading to a dramatic end (4,3)
2 The end of education? (9,6)
3 Nothing of an ancient city belongs to us (4)
4 One following the route of endless decorative pattern (6)
5 Ascertain amount of cooked veal that's acceptable before tea-break (8)
6 Not always striking according to the circumstances (3-3-4)
7 Tourist attraction possibly never seen (4,4,7)
8 More fleshy-sounding space traveller (6)
13 Happening to be with posh friend at long last (10)
16 The gentry take so much trouble to find a watch (6-2)

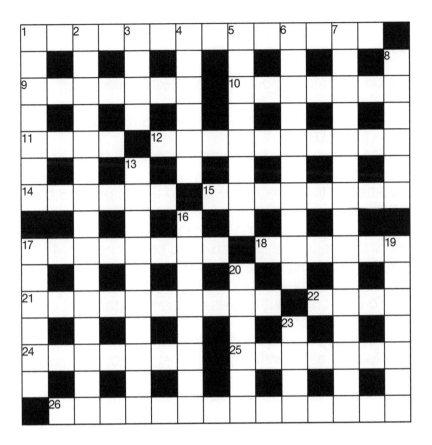

17 Dandy oriental heard was a fine specimen (6)
19 Mischievousness of removing rouge lines (7)
20 A chunk is for an Egyptian god (6)
23 Branch member (4)

78

ACROSS

1 Do the French provide a job seeker's allowance? (4)

3 One who comes out against an examination for a worker (10)

8 Place where one might make a bad mistake when in company (6)

9 Attempt to get more the second time around (3,5)

10 Seeing a problem for one I stir up (6)

11 I'm taking two articles to a first rate copier (8)

12 Sort of relationship which could be on or off (4-4)

14 This plant just came up! (4)

16 Go slow in the centre of this city (4)

18 To be more beautiful was of less importance about last December (8)

19 Put a pigeon in a old cannon (8)

20 Roughly agree with first man that it's not very much (6)

21 An awful crisis causes bloomers to be made (8)

22 Horses sound as though they're refusing (6)

23 Normal gossip, but coming from off shore perhaps (7,3)

24 A square works the best (4)

DOWN

1 Received letters from him, although he was unfaithful... (8)

2 ...and a letter about your first door frame (8)

3 Angry about having to go to the other side... (5,4)

4 ...in spite of being able to sit down (15)

5 Surprise opening against the French (7)

6 A tin so placed to hold a prickly plant (8)

7 Purport to be a singer (5)

13 The pieces cut off – or put on! (9)

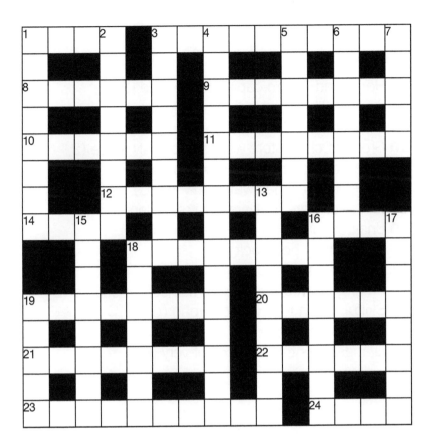

15 Roll out some sort of steel shoe – not the left one (8)

16 Musician gets another roasting (8)

17 Has fixed ideas, the boss sees difficulties (8)

18 About a thousand in support, that's first class (7)

19 This priest is a hundred soon! (5)

79

ACROSS

1 Henry and I go to capital horse race (8)
6 Declaim liturgy, going round city (6)
9 Bold as brass? (6)
10 Group of characters writers endlessly reuse (8)
11 Do a stunt badly and be conspicuous (5,3)
12 Observe what melt-water now is? (6)
13 Joints for fliers that are really excellent (3,4,5)
16 Unaided, and with only one arm? (6-6)
19 An earl may be struck (6)
21 Placed at duties, perhaps (8)
23 Putting down of the French subject for debate (8)
24 Skilful Italian follows tricky road (6)
25 A dandy, too (2,4)
26 Evangelist enthusiastic? Not very (8)

DOWN

2 Add some fizz – taking a long time, note (6)
3 Number of apostles act over Buddhist sect (5)
4 Cannot see translation into Chinese (9)
5 After quiet, disconcert with chatter (7)
6 Trip only includes one city (5)
7 Conservative was quick to be disciplined (9)
8 One digging for plate (8)
13 Tense supporter of high-wire act (9)
14 After accident, trace skid to minor road (9)
15 Enjoy head's portrait (8)
17 A right to dig up roads to weapon store (7)
18 I snore horribly when older (6)
20 Dentist's practice? (5)
22 Missile arrives – that hurt! (5)

ACROSS

1 In a religious house it takes precedence (8)
5 Note Celia composed in Erse (6)
9 Eponymous winner of the 1981 Grand National (8)
10 Jug couple presented to single child (6)
11 Postscript written by the chiropodist (8)
12 Stick the poster in this spot (6)
14 Godly man speaking – but with difficulty (10)
18 Receive notice from the sherry salesman (3,3,4)
22 Article about a fortified wine (6)
23 Wear ties knotted unusually, so to speak (2,2,4)
24 Lady with a halo (6)
25 Column I covered with gypsum (8)
26 Made Greene break a promise (6)
27 Scheme by fellow of mournful nature (8)

DOWN

1 Spend about 101 francs to restore calm (6)
2 Quarrelling with one after another (2,1,3)
3 Feel sorry for keeping soldiers cooped up (6)
4 Criticised when driven to work (4,2,4)
6 Contracted to build a viaduct before 1st December (8)
7 Leninist ordered to tap the telephone (6,2)
8 Meet criminal by the roadside (8)
13 There's merchandise to sell, but it's not moving (5-5)
15 A fish repeatedly served in seaweed jelly (4-4)
16 Don swept out when made to resign (4,4)
17 The Church Militant is winning (8)
19 Stress family pedigree (6)
20 Arrange to deliver a bench (6)
21 Redstart, wading bird showing sense of loss (6)

ANSWERS

1

Across

1 Freedom
5 Rail-car
9 One up on
10 Interim
11 Negotiate
12 Ravel
13 Esses
15 Discerned
17 Disappear
19 Extra
22 Salvo
23 Anatomist
25 Estates
26 Elector
27 Deserve
28 Starred

Down

1 Flounce
2 Emerges
3 Depot
4 Manhandle
5 Rhine
6 Intercede
7 Caravan
8 Rumpled
14 Supporter
16 Streamers
17 Distend
18 Salutes
20 Twister
21 Altered
23 Aisle
24 Opera

2

Across

1 Half nelson
6 Coop
9 Legit
10 Time-lapse
12 Toy with an idea
14 Nurtured
15 Signet
17 Lesson
19 Eldorado
21 Startling news
24 Manhattan
25 Larch
26 Nary
27 Power-plant

Down

1 Helm
2 Lighter
3 Not my cup of tea
4 Latticed
5 Oomph
7 Oppidan
8 Precaution
11 Land in one's lap
13 Englishman
16 Elegance
18 Stainer
20 Austria
22 Intro
23 Chit

3

Across

1 Opposer
5 Details
9 Theorem
10 Traffic
11 Chevalier
12 Nonce
13 Latch
15 Dartboard
17 Meandered
19 Ether
22 Rhoda
23 Spearhead
25 Amongst
26 Topside
27 Despair
28 Resigns

Down

1 Optical
2 Present
3 Syria
4 Remainder
5 Doter
6 Trainable
7 Infanta
8 Succeed
14 Hydrangea
16 Red-letter
17 Mermaid
18 Amorous
20 Heeling
21 Redress
23 Sitar
24 Ropes

4

Across
8 Ephemera
9 Orange
10 Nim
11 Libretti
12 Binary
13 Charles Kingsley
15 Cardiff
18 Stealer
21 The Marx Brothers
24 Cleric
25 Gallants
26 Ana
27 Realms
28 Incident

Down
1 Uppish
2 Bearer
3 Weather forecast
4 Panicky
5 Combination lock
6 Magnesia
7 Aggrieve
14 Ayr
16 Achilles
17 Demurely
19 Lie
20 Abigail
22 Hoards
23 Rating

5

Across
1 Horns
4 Angelica
10 Sustain
11 Violate
12 Pits
13 Sorry
14 Bird
17 Phosphorescent
19 Contraventions
22 Mote
23 Jelly
24 Vera
27 & 30 I haven't a clue
28 Nirvana
29 Treatise
30 See 27

Down
1 Hosepipe
2 Risotto
3 Span
5 Never Never Land
6 Eton
7 Iranian
8 Amend
9 In loco parentis
15 Spots
16 Acute
18 Escapade
20 Outrage
21 Overall
22 Moist
25 Seat
26 Area

6

Across
1 Single
5 Castaway
9 Paranormal
10 Till
11 Honolulu
12 Thrown
13 Brag
15 Treading
18 Painless
19 Weep
21 Myopia
23 Rooftops
25 Bass
26 Out of sorts
27 Research
28 Tattoo

Down
2 Idaho
3 Glamorgan
4 Exodus
5 Come up to scratch
6 Splutter
7 Aster
8 Allowance
14 Ready-made
16 Do without
17 Belabour
20 Wolfit
22 Paste
24 Patio

7

Across
- **1** Rustling
- **9** Outclass
- **10** Idea
- **11** Dutch courage
- **13** Startled
- **15** Lapsed
- **16** Swot
- **17** Goner
- **18** Owed
- **20** Accrue
- **21** Recounts
- **23** Does one's best
- **26** Iago
- **27** Returned
- **28** Absentee

Down
- **2** Undertow
- **3** Trade returns
- **4** Instal
- **5** Goth
- **6** Stroller
- **7** Lama
- **8** Ascended
- **12** Reproduction
- **14** Diner
- **16** Standard
- **17** Gleaning
- **19** Entangle
- **22** Cheers
- **24** Efts
- **25** Soda

8

Across
- **1** High-flier
- **9** Troppo
- **10** Bartender
- **11** Impend
- **12** Vacillate
- **13** Stolen
- **17** Bit
- **19** Acquire currency
- **20** Tab
- **21** Staffa
- **25** Offensive
- **26** Bleach
- **27** Cut across
- **28** Needle
- **29** Statesman

Down
- **2** In a way
- **3** Hattie
- **4** Lonely
- **5** Electrical fault
- **6** Premature
- **7** Appellant
- **8** Golden-eye
- **14** Waistband
- **15** Square-leg
- **16** Difficult
- **17** Bet
- **18** Tub
- **22** Levant
- **23** Osiris
- **24** Avesta

9

Across
- **7** Periscope
- **8** Ingot
- **10** Altitude
- **11** Drowse
- **12** Inca
- **13** Landlord
- **15** Groused
- **17** Trade-in
- **20** Bearskin
- **22** Gasp
- **25** Prison
- **26** Port erin
- **27** Found
- **28** Screaming

Down
- **1** Wells
- **2** Minion
- **3** Accurate
- **4** Appeals
- **5** Ennobled
- **6** Constrain
- **9** Aden
- **14** Greenroom
- **16** Uprising
- **18** Regarded
- **19** Inspect
- **21** Kind
- **23** Steamy
- **24** Fiend

10

Across
1 Orderlies
8 Chief of police
11 Mote
12 Midas
13 Tour
16 Smoking
17 Dustman
18 Nelsons
20 Scandal
21 Last
22 Babel
23 Stun
26 Hercule Poirot
27 Butterfly

Down
2 Reed
3 Eroding
4 Lapland
5 Eels
6 Ghetto blaster
7 Accommodation
9 Amusingly
10 Front line
14 Ripon
15 Islay
19 Scarlet
20 Sleeper
24 Ecru
25 Bill

11

Across
1 Fourth dimension
9 Crimson
10 Reactor
11 Iteration
12 Sigma
13 Nursery
15 Radiate
17 Prattle
19 Torrent
21 Owing
23 Adumbrate
25 Extract
26 Adamant
27 Second childhood

Down
1 Faction
2 Unite
3 Testament
4 Density
5 Mariner
6 Nears
7 Integrate
8 Narrate
14 Realistic
16 Dartboard
17 Process
18 Elastic
19 Tsunami
20 Treated
22 Grain
24 Alamo

12

Across
1 Campaigner
6 Asks
10 Onset
11 Elucidate
12 Clement
13 The flat
14 Ground stroke
18 Play with fire
21 Castled
23 Routine
24 On the side
25 Pride
26 Slew
27 In stitches

Down
1 Choice
2 Master
3 As the crow flies
4 Great-aunt
5 Erupt
7 Stallion
8 Sweet pea
9 Like it or lump it
15 Deferment
16 Specious
17 Cassette
19 Finish
20 Begets
22 Deign

13

Across
1 Campus
4 Estimate
9 Rarely
10 Straw-hat
12 Iota
13 Grass
14 Knee
17 Game of chance
20 Music-teacher
23 Acer
24 Igloo
25 Dean
28 All clear
29 Head-on
30 Turnover
31 Bridge

Down
1 Carriage
2 Maritime
3 Ugly
5 Satisfaction
6 Iran
7 At hand
8 Either
11 Cracking pace
15 Bogus
16 Ocean
18 Threaded
19 Ordnance
21 Savant
22 Peeler
26 Alto
27 Weir

14

Across
1 Close to home
10 Mimed
11 Rembrandt
12 Knowledge
13 Neigh
14 Newark
16 Peerless
18 Jaundice
20 Abloom
23 Coded
24 Accordant
26 Ernestine
27 Oakum
28 Engaged tone

Down
2 Limbo
3 Saddler
4 Tirade
5 Hampered
6 Mariner
7 Smoking jacket
8 Antihero
9 At the same time
15 Wounding
17 Sciatica
19 Dodgson
21 Burn out
22 Scheme
25 Ask in

15

Across
1 Reappear
5 Potent
9 Cardigan
10 Astern
12 Stalemate
13 Ruche
14 Cast
16 Reissue
19 Dropper
21 Rage
24 Exile
25 Appeasers
27 Enamel
28 Moderate
29 Trendy
30 Dead heat

Down
1 Recess
2 Abroad
3 Pride
4 Adamant
6 Observing
7 Exercise
8 Tendered
11 Bear
15 Apprehend
17 Adherent
18 Nominate
20 Real
21 Reprove
22 Beware
23 Assent
26 Amend

16

Across

1 Herbivorous
9 Faro
10 Micawberish
11 Pain
14 Opulent
16 Leather
17 Throw
18 Flog
19 Stud
20 Sneak
22 Eroding
23 Liaison
24 Pelt
28 Opinion poll
29 Lark
30 Streakiness

Down

2 Eric
3 Beat
4 Vibrant
5 Rare
6 Unscrew
7 Parachutist
8 Downgrading
12 Toffee-apple
13 Eurodollars
15 Thing
16 Local
20 Snippet
21 Kinfolk
25 Once
26 Spin
27 Alas

17

Across

1 Shaddock
5 Hemmed
9 Athenian
10 Strife
12 Personate
13 Notes
14 Dial
16 Opinion
19 Romance
21 Wand
24 Steer
25 Beefeater
27 Reigns
28 Stagnate
29 Eschew
30 Tenement

Down

1 Snappy
2 Adhere
3 Dingo
4 Chagall
6 Extension
7 Maintain
8 Dressing
11 Peso
15 Ignorance
17 Preserve
18 Amnesiac
20 Elba
21 Wrestle
22 At ease
23 Ardent
26 Eagre

18

Across

1 Second childhood
9 Inn sign
10 Chiffon
11 Woad
12 Quail
13 Scar
16 Tuscany
17 Generic
18 Turn out
21 Current
23 Emmy
24 Divan
25 Vice
28 In limbo
29 El Greco
30 Error of judgment

Down

1 Swim with the tide
2 Canvass
3 Naif
4 Century
5 Itching
6 Drip
7 Officer
8 Don't rock the boat
14 Manor
15 Snort
19 Rambler
20 Tail off
21 Chateau
22 Evil eye
26 Emir
27 Agog

19

Across

1 Near enough
9 Here
10 Refinement
11 Comics
12 Saddles
15 Decline
16 Sward
17 Owns
18 Limb
19 Magog
21 Cresset
22 Layette
24 Malawi
27 Agreements
28 Side
29 Second team

Down

2 Ever
3 Railed
4 Needles
5 Uses
6 Hitched
7 Recidivist
8 Reassemble
12 Scotch mist
13 Dinner lady
14 Sweat
15 Drool
19 Menials
20 Galleon
23 Except
25 Eric
26 Etna

20

Across

1 Madam
4 Constant
8 Revolver
9 Epiphany
11 Sedated
13 Relapsing
15 Made things worse
18 New Mexico
21 Tactful
22 Steerage
24 Paddling
25 Tartaric
26 Gigot

Down

1 Markswoman
2 Dividend
3 Militant
4 Core
5 Slap-up
6 Alkali
7 Tony
10 Polyglot
12 Draining
14 Green light
16 Watchdog
17 Ruffling
19 Weeper
20 Europa
22 Skit
23 Epic

21

Across

1 Head-on crash
7 Foretop
8 Matting
10 Enoch
11 Stanchion
12 Candour
14 Several
15 Lockjaw
18 Macadam
20 Articular
21 Dozen
22 Emeriti
23 Ideally
24 Denominator

Down

1 Harpoon
2 Aitch
3 Opposer
4 Compass
5 Anticivic
6 Hairier
7 French leave
9 Gentlemanly
13 Objection
16 Cathead
17 William
18 Martian
19 Dazzler
21 Dwelt

22

Across
1 Robert Peel
9 Stye
10 Stirrup-cup
11 Lusaka
12 Candles
15 Antigua
16 Dosed
17 Ergo
18 Mini
19 Debit
21 Settler
22 Shotgun
24 Carafe
27 Real Madrid
28 Kiss
29 Seamstress

Down
2 Opts
3 Earned
4 Touched
5 Etch
6 Lapland
7 Strangling
8 Reparation
12 Cheesecake
13 Nightdress
14 Sober
15 Aegis
19 Deserts
20 Thermos
23 Tender
25 Lava
26 Miss

23

Across
1 Long John Silver
9 Battier
10 Insects
11 UFOs
12 Percentage
14 Smarmy
15 Relevant
17 Testator
18 Remiss
21 Wordsworth
22 Once
24 Grinder
25 Elegant
26 Near the knuckle

Down
1 Labours
2 National Service
3 Jail
4 Hornet
5 Stitches
6 Los Angeles
7 Exclamation mark
8 Assent
13 Ambassador
16 Gomorrah
17 Towage
19 Sheathe
20 Streak
23 Menu

24

Across
1 Sacramento
6 Snap
10 Chant
11 Readdress
12 Chop-chop
13 Assam
15 Factory
17 Dickens
19 Tragedy
21 Red tape
22 Egg on
24 Restrain
27 On the nail
28 Brace
29 Kind
30 Impediment

Down
1 Sack
2 Cha-cha-cha
3 Act up
4 Earthly
5 Trapped
7 Needs
8 Past master
9 Advanced
14 Off the hook
16 Oleander
18 Eradicate
20 Yard-arm
21 Resolve
23 Got on
25 Rabbi
26 Best

25

Across
1 Loots
4 Daughters
8 Offer
9 Unlearned
11 Eons
12 Plant
13 Pike
16 Illogicalness
19 Freudian slips
20 Apse
22 Hitch
23 Swap
26 Derring-do
27 Hairy
28 Sleepwalk
29 Tweed

Down
1 Loose-leaf
2 Offensive
3 Serf
4 Double glazing
5 Hear
6 Ennui
7 Sedge
10 Longcase clock
14 Blade
15 Plain
17 Erstwhile
18 Sharp-eyed
20 Andes
21 Surge
24 Wisp
25 Whit

26

Across
1 Scrapers
5 Strove
9 Organist
10 Castle
12 Gladstone
13 Split
14 Page
16 Aroused
19 Relates
21 Anti
24 Scamp
25 Racehorse
27 Braise
28 Currying
29 Ration
30 Stampede

Down
1 Slough
2 Rag-day
3 Punts
4 Restore
6 Transport
7 Outclass
8 Eventide
11 Vera
15 Antipasto
17 Crossbar
18 Pleasant
20 Sort
21 Account
22 Orpine
23 Meagre
26 Harem

27

Across
1 Spring back
6 Awed
10 Lunch
11 Tailoress
12 Squelch
13 Pointer
14 Emerald green
18 Commandeered
21 Nurture
23 Apology
24 Piecemeal
25 Trash
26 Seta
27 Drawbridge

Down
1 Splash
2 Run out
3 No half
   measures
4 Butchered
5 Chimp
7 Wrestler
8 Desiring
9 Roving reporter
15 Lie fallow
16 Schnapps
17 Emergent
19 Howard
20 Lychee
22 Emeer

28

Across

7 Battersea
8 Frail
10 Combined
11 Ladder
12 Leda
13 Eastward
15 Insight
17 Pot-shot
20 Aesthete
22 Dash
25 Owlets
26 Rearming
27 On tap
28 Punchline

Down

1 Wagon
2 Stable
3 Bran-mash
4 Seedbed
5 Bradawls
6 Fireproof
9 Plus
14 Underwent
16 In the bag
18 Ordnance
19 Ferrous
21 Erse
23 Sample
24 Inane

29

Across

1 Trail-blazer
9 Bookmaker
10 Dicky
11 Titled
12 Charcoal
13 Noggin
15 Nuisance
18 Flagging
19 Taurus
21 Cottager
23 Flower
26 Loser
27 Storm cone
28 Ladies' night

Down

1 Tibetan
2 About
3 Lumbering
4 Like
5 Zero hour
6 Radar
7 Royal we
8 Schooner
14 Giantess
16 Stableman
17 Unversed
18 Faculty
20 Surfeit
22 April
24 Wrong
25 Cope

30

Across

1 Pack-drill
6 Model
9 Clamant
10 Inanimate
11 Disease
12 Imagery
13 Plain-clothes man
18 Diderot
20 Missive
22 Disdained
23 Alewife
24 Toddy
25 Teenagers

Down

1 Picked up
2 Charisma
3 Dharma
4 In time
5 Loyalist
6 Meditate
7 Debate
8 Likely
14 Normally
15 Latinist
16 Main line
17 Needless
18 Deduct
19 Dashed
20 Madame
21 Seneca

31

Across
 1 Accusations
 8 Forestation
11 Idas
12 Note
13 Intense
15 Relater
16 Sager
17 Trip
18 Fast
19 React
21 Regular
22 Hold-all
23 Silk
26 Pure
27 Enterprises
28 Proposition

Down
 2 Coos
 3 Useless
 4 Anti
 5 Intoner
 6 Noon
 7 Miniaturist
 8 Farthingale
 9 Nostradamus
10 Deerstalker
14 Eater
15 Reach
19 Raise up
20 Tourist
24 Knar
25 Spas
26 Peso

32

Across
 1 Illiterate
 6 Polo
10 Corot
11 Amendment
12 Nearside
13 Plate
15 Execute
17 Seismal
19 Testing
21 Pandean
22 Pasta
24 Lollipop
27 Dreamland
28 Irish
29 Sole
30 Stonemason

Down
 1 Inch
 2 Largeness
 3 Tutor
 4 Realise
 5 Theseus
 7 Opera
 8 Outselling
 9 Adoption
14 Centipedes
16 Up in arms
18 Mnemonics
20 Gallant
21 Paladin
23 Spell
25 Idiom
26 Shun

33

Across
 1 Fall through
 7 Egret
 8 Awestruck
10 Sky-blue
11 Elation
12 Lehar
13 Brainwash
16 Means test
18 Cocoa
19 Veteran
22 Turn out
23 Directrix
24 Timid
25 Smokescreen

Down
 1 Forsythia
 2 Littler
 3 Traceable
 4 Reeve
 5 Up-train
 6 Houri
 7 Easily moved
 9 Kind-hearted
14 Antitoxic
15 Anchorman
17 Sirocco
18 Curette
20 Torus
21 Norse

34

Across
1 In range
5 Shindig
9 Eugenic
10 Brassie
11 Almshouse
12 Gouda
13 Tunis
15 Tolerable
17 Despaired
19 Leave
22 Set-to
23 Sheerness
25 Austere
26 Message
27 Fly-half
28 Nankeen

Down
1 Inexact
2 Regimen
3 Ninth
4 Encounter
5 Sable
6 Inaugural
7 Disturb
8 Grenade
14 Soap opera
16 Ladies' man
17 Distaff
18 Satisfy
20 Average
21 Eastern
23 Shelf
24 Risen

35

Across
1 Thunderclap
10 Rumba
11 Never mind
12 Condenser
13 Comma
14 Nicety
16 Platonic
18 Ethereal
20 Flayed
23 Terms
24 Avalanche
26 Ownership
27 Lapse
28 Reinstating

Down
2 Human
3 Nearest
4 Ernest
5 Cover-all
6 Apricot
7 Preconception
8 Pin money
9 Advanced level
15 Coherent
17 Marathon
19 Reserve
21 Leaflet
22 Carpet
25 Capon

36

Across
1 Bed of roses
6 Camp
9 Refer
10 Set fire to
12 Clear one's name
14 Androgen
15 Object
17 Abased
19 Porridge
21 At the same time
24 Keep faith
25 Amman
26 Nosh
27 Rattletrap

Down
1 Bard
2 Defaced
3 Forget oneself
4 Observer
5 Eaten
7 Average
8 Properties
11 Insubordinate
13 Banana skin
16 Somewhat
18 Actress
20 Dreamer
22 Avila
23 Snap

37

Across

1 Romeo and Juliet
9 Upstart
10 Panacea
11 Once
12 Lounge bars
14 Solent
15 Acid rain
17 Scimitar
18 Minima
21 Prevention
22 Anna
24 Letitia
25 Emanate
26 Practical joker

Down

1 Raucous
2 Musical director
3 Oval
4 Nation
5 Japonica
6 Linseed oil
7 Exclamation mark
8 Parson
13 Antiseptic
16 Pastrami
17 Supple
19 Amateur
20 Bodega
23 Hadj

38

Across

1 Casts off
5 Stowed
9 Evermore
10 Drills
11 Tireless
12 Parole
14 Barometers
18 Apostolate
22 Edmund
23 Insolent
24 Auntie
25 Gingerly
26 Emerge
27 Agitated

Down

1 Cheats
2 Sherry
3 Sample
4 Forestalls
6 Threaten
7 Walkover
8 Dispense
13 Portending
15 Base rate
16 Commence
17 Stinting
19 Sought
20 Learnt
21 Stayed

39

Across

1 Comedy
4 Stock-car
10 Registrar
11 Mimic
12 Lateran
13 Watered
14 Sandy
15 Conflict
18 Bandanna
20 Tetra
23 Cuticle
25 Acrobat
26 Tacky
27 Totaliser
28 Redouble
29 Byword

Down

1 Careless
2 Megaton
3 Destroyed
5 Throwing a party
6 Comet
7 Cambric
8 Recede
9 Transcendental
16 Literally
17 Captured
19 Antacid
21 Tabasco
22 Scoter
24 Coypu

40

Across
1 Needle matches
10 Overdue
11 Useless
12 Play
13 Delta
14 Viva
17 Sits out
18 Donegal
19 Perhaps
22 Minutes
24 Idle
25 Afire
26 Firm
29 Teacher
30 Cartoon
31 Getting on a bit

Down
2 Elegant
3 Dido
4 Element
5 Abutted
6 Cues
7 Evening
8 Compass points
9 Establishment
15 Total
16 Inane
20 Release
21 Saffron
22 Morocco
23 Tripoli
27 Whit
28 Proa

41

Across
1 Animal Farm
6 Left
10 Aspic
11 Shoeblack
12 Set aside
13 Abets
15 Sustain
17 Shampoo
19 Andante
21 Retrace
22 Waver
24 Badinage
27 Lucrative
28 Rooks
29 Ella
30 Head keeper

Down
1 Agar
2 Impressed
3 Accra
4 Fashion
5 Rioters
7 Erase
8 Takes cover
9 Abradant
14 Oscar wilde
16 Abnormal
18 Playgroup
20 Ebb-tide
21 Redhead
23 Vocal
25 Nurse
26 User

42

Across
1 Coward
4 Push-over
9 Savage
10 Old world
12 Lore
13 Fence
14 Call
17 Tunnel vision
20 Pound of flesh
23 Load
24 Taper
25 Harm
28 New blood
29 Retail
30 Hay fever
31 Rhodes

Down
1 Cast lots
2 Wavering
3 Rage
5 Ugly customer
6 Howl
7 Vernal
8 Riddle
11 Heavens above
15 Below
16 Corfu
18 Legal aid
19 Shambles
21 Flinch
22 Galway
26 Clue
27 Beth

43

Across
1 Yardstick
6 Music
9 Cossack
10 Ingenious
11 Inuring
12 Trellis
13 Game set and match
18 Yew-tree
20 Repiner
22 Relenting
23 Opposed
24 Run up
25 Throwaway

Down
1 Yachting
2 Residuum
3 Scampi
4 Inking
5 Kingston
6 Moonbeam
7 School
8 Crisis
14 Spring up
15 Teeniest
16 Tenon-saw
17 Heraldry
18 Yorker
19 Wilton
20 Rigour
21 Pawpaw

44

Across
1 Clear the air
7 Persist
8 Modicum
10 Roost
11 Anarchist
12 Enticed
14 Shingle
15 Hiccups
18 Hangdog
20 Upsetting
21 Gusto
22 Epitome
23 Teenage
24 Tam-o'-shanter

Down
1 Car port
2 Edict
3 Rutland
4 Hymnals
5 Addiction
6 Rocking
7 Porterhouse
9 Mother Goose
13 Courtroom
16 Casuist
17 Shivers
18 High tea
19 Despair
21 Great

45

Across
1 & 5 Fast and furious
9 Regroup
10 Bristle
11 Hairslide
12 Forum
13 & 15 Right and proper
17 Damascene
19 Elbow
22 Tessa
23 Test cases
25 Italian
26 Sausage
27 Spanner
28 Press on

Down
1 & 17 down Further details
2 Signing
3 Atoms
4 Duplicate
5 Fibre
6 Reinforce
7 Outcrop
8 Steamer
14 Tasmanian
16 Dresses up
17 *See 1 across*
18 Mascara
20 Bus pass
21 Western
23 Tenor
24 Cruse

46

Across
1 Carried weight
7 Het up
8 Rearrange
9 Lowland
10 Abalone
11 Idyll
12 Cracksman
14 Test pilot
17 Ached
19 Epigram
21 Embargo
22 Antipodes
23 Truss
24 Long time no see

Down
1 Cut away
2 Raphael
3 Diana
4 Earmark
5 Gunroom
6 The penny drops
7 Hole-in-the-wall
8 Radical
13 Artless
15 Stilton
16 Parapet
17 Arbutus
18 Hirsute
20 Madam

47

Across
1 Guidepost
9 Othello
10 Scorers
11 Average
12 Beanfeast
14 Loyalist
15 Unless
17 Censure
20 Errant
23 Distance
25 Addresser
26 Reached
27 Overtip
28 Extract
29 Sacrilege

Down
2 Unclean
3 Derange
4 Perverse
5 Tomato
6 Shoemaker
7 Alsatia
8 Lowestoft
13 Slashed
15 Unadorned
16 Scrapheap
18 Reprover
19 Esparto
21 Rostral
22 Needing
24 Cadets

48

Across
1 Philatelist
9 Hoodlum
10 Anthem
12 Plaudit
13 Theatre
14 Irony
15 Brasserie
17 Tawdriest
20 Clout
22 Ringlet
24 Melodic
25 Pliant
26 Terrace
27 Pret-a-porter

Down
2 Holiday
3 Limitable
4 Toast
5 Letters
6 Sweater
7 Shoplifters
8 Potato
11 Receptacles
16 Altimeter
18 Wangler
19 Reliant
20 Calorie
21 Ordeal
23 Tot up

49

Across
1 Aramaic
5 Chelsea
9 Dwelt
10 Blow-torch
11 Relentless
12 Oner
14 Madame Bovary
18 Apple-blossom
21 Acid
22 Stepsister
25 Continent
26 Irate
27 Dullest
28 Leg bail

Down
1 Adders
2 Age-old
3 Attenuated
4 Cabal
5 Cloisters
6 Elts
7 Sirenian
8 Ashtrays
13 Colonising
15 Allotment
16 Balanced
17 Optional
19 Strata
20 Ordeal
23 Petal
24 Tide

50

Across
1 Doric
4 Lipstick
8 Villager
9 Attitude
11 Napping
13 Abasement
15 Indian rope-trick
18 Narcissus
21 Tallies
22 Croutons
24 Carapace
25 Chestnut
26 Knead

Down
1 Divination
2 Relapsed
3 Charisma
4 Lira
5 Strife
6 Insure
7 Kite
10 Trappist
12 Garrison
14 Take as read
16 Tailback
17 Indicate
19 Rookie
20 Intact
22 Chic
23 Scot

51

Across
1 Forced landing
10 Oppress
11 Open-air
12 Lieu
13 Abate
14 Rasp
17 Wise men
18 Eyeball
19 Non-stop
22 Ottoman
24 Watt
25 Stays
26 Asti
29 Norwich
30 Proviso
31 Electric light

Down
2 Orpheus
3 Co-ed
4 Dustbin
5 Apostle
6 Duel
7 Niagara
8 Following wind
9 Grappling iron
15 Smith
16 Delta
20 Natural
21 Pitcher
22 Olympic
23 Messiah
27 Disc
28 Topi

52

Across
1 Stager
4 Cup of tea
8 Pallid
9 Anchored
10 Radioing
11 Suture
12 Intaglio
13 Ogress
15 Armpit
18 Slippage
20 Admire
21 Effacing
23 Hotplate
24 Rhodes
25 Recovery
26 Easily

Down
1 Super
2 Galliwasp
3 Redhill
4 Change of scenery
5 Picasso
6 Torture
7 Addressee
12 In a lather
14 Rapacious
16 Mimetic
17 Teenage
19 In force
22 Gusty

53

Across
1 Persistent
9 Rude
10 Arbitrator
11 Resist
12 Hearing
15 Inflate
16 Giant
17 Ramp
18 Vile
19 Ceres
21 Artisan
22 Request
24 Italic
27 Architects
28 Tuck
29 Eisenstein

Down
2 Earl
3 Shiver
4 Serving
5 Efts
6 Torrent
7 Ruminative
8 Settlement
12 Herbalists
13 Admittance
14 Given
15 Infer
19 Cascade
20 Section
23 Unrest
25 Acis
26 Etui

54

Across
1 Perfect pitch
8 Classes
9 Ambrose
11 Despite
12 Trouble
13 Madge
14 Decameron
16 Ancestral
19 Ought
21 Arrival
23 Set fair
24 Daemons
25 Italian
26 Storytellers

Down
1 Praised
2 Restive
3 East ender
4 Trait
5 In bloom
6 Clobber
7 Academy award
10 Eternity ring
15 Celestial
17 Current
18 Saviour
19 Outrage
20 Gravies
22 Liszt

55

Across

7 Eliminate
8 Sheen
10 Nineteen
11 Minded
12 Aden
13 Attempts
15 Galatea
17 Asinine
20 Madeline
22 Away
25 Fiasco
26 Endorsed
27 Depot
28 Naturists

Down

1 Flair
2 Impend
3 Antennae
4 Etonian
5 Chinamen
6 Repeating
9 Emit
14 Parasites
16 Aversion
18 Stand out
19 General
21 Iron
23 Afraid
24 Set-to

56

Across

1 Pan-pipes
9 Agitator
10 Kiln
11 Cross section
13 Harassed
15 Exeunt
16 Fend
17 Minus
18 Apse
20 Annual
21 Reacting
23 Staying power
26 Unit
27 Milanese
28 Misspent

Down

2 Alienate
3 Punch and Judy
4 Patois
5 Says
6 Timeless
7 Etui
8 Brunette
12 The last trump
14 Donor
16 Fearsome
17 Malinger
19 Sanction
22 Always
24 Ally
25 Poem

57

Across

1 Beseech
5 Dynamos
9 Ovation
10 Nigeria
11 Entrances
12 Thief
13 Darts
15 Five-a-side
17 Narcissus
19 Epoch
22 Mated
23 Editorial
25 Scoring
26 Umbrage
27 Sweater
28 Entails

Down

1 Book-end
2 Starter
3 Evita
4 Handcuffs
5 Dines
6 Negotiate
7 Martini
8 Snaffle
14 Spindrift
16 Vestibule
17 Nemesis
18 Rat-hole
20 Origami
21 Holders
23 Elgar
24 Orbit

58

Across
1 Hop skip and jump
9 Traduced
10 Siren
12 Hugh
13 Classicist
15 Cannibal
16 Scythe
18 Toledo
20 Couscous
23 On the cards
24 Stem
26 Prior
27 Breather
28 Know one's onions

Down
2 Paragon
3 Kudu
4 Peculiar
5 Nodose
6 Just in case
7 Marxist
8 And then some
11 Shock-troops
14 Middlebrow
17 Boldness
19 Lothian
21 On the go
22 Carbon
25 Stan

59

Across
1 Streaker
5 Spirit
9 Repaired
10 Drover
12 Pulverise
13 Purse
14 Pine
16 Marengo
19 Scratch
21 Disc
24 Rodeo
25 Downright
27 Eats up
28 Ignorant
29 Sunder
30 Drabness

Down
1 Scrape
2 Ripple
3 Alice
4 Eremite
6 Perspires
7 Reverent
8 Turned on
11 Term
15 Introduce
17 Usurpers
18 Crediton
20 Hide
21 Dowager
22 Agnate
23 States
26 Rhomb

60

Across
1 Indicative
6 Utah
10 Canal
11 Non-smoker
12 Cannabis
13 Hosed
15 Eyesore
17 Nascent
19 Arsenal
21 Cashier
22 Epsom
24 Nainsook
27 Entangled
28 Acute
29 Tort
30 Anatomists

Down
1 Inch
2 Dungarees
3 Colon
4 Tenable
5 Venison
7 Takes
8 Hereditary
9 Emphasis
14 Defacement
16 Ointment
18 Epilogues
20 Lanolin
21 Chindit
23 Sitar
25 Swarm
26 Reis

61

Across
1 Bus pass
5 Visitor
9 Splitting
10 Arras
11 Doyen
12 Talk round
13 Sensation
16 Spine
17 Hop it
18 Free agent
20 Mousetrap
23 Ogive
25 Rhino
26 Acquitted
27 Mummery
28 Eagerly

Down
1 Besides
2 Splay
3 Attendant
4 Swift
5 Vigilante
6 Stair
7 Turquoise
8 Residue
14 Neptunium
15 Infirmary
16 Shadowing
17 Humdrum
19 Tuesday
21 Evoke
22 Pique
24 Inter

62

Across
1 Curator
5 Brigand
9 Unguent
10 Distant
11 Broadside
12 Reach
13 Resin
15 Inspected
17 Colleague
19 Taper
22 Ictus
23 Get across
25 Perjury
26 No sweat
27 Related
28 Reserve

Down
1 Clubber
2 Regions
3 Tweed
4 Retailing
5 Badge
6 Insurgent
7 Adamant
8 Ditched
14 Needs must
16 Sweetener
17 Clipper
18 Lateral
20 Pioneer
21 Rosette
23 Guyed
24 Casts

63

Across
8 Shoehorn
9 Unfair
10 Gas
11 Oriental
12 Shifty
13 Railway stations
15 Splints
18 Drilled
21 Flirtatiousness
24 Oregon
25 Eventide
26 Tot
27 Statue
28 Tottered

Down
1 Chorea
2 Befell
3 Portrait painter
4 English
5 Russian roulette
6 Official
7 Distance
14 Ill
16 Polarity
17 Irrigate
19 Lie
20 Biretta
22 Nether
23 Sodden

64

Across
1 Enterprise
6 Talc
10 Lowed
11 Persevere
12 Scarcity
13 Order
15 Raiment
17 Dormant
19 Worsted
21 Spencer
22 Rumba
24 Lavished
27 Direction
28 Reims
29 Erne
30 Breakwater

Down
1 Eels
2 Towncrier
3 Rider
4 Repaint
5 Strayed
7 Amend
8 Clearstory
9 Recourse
14 Drawbridge
16 Entrance
18 Alchemist
20 Dallier
21 Savanna
23 Moron
25 Screw
26 Tsar

65

Across
1 Floating capital
9 Resonance
10 At sea
11 Toluene
12 Rat race
13 Emu
14 Preston
17 Portico
19 Evident
22 Baronet
24 Use
25 Remoter
26 Sidecar
28 Not on
29 Imitation
30 Exchange letters

Down
1 First appearance
2 Ousel
3 Tangent
4 Nankeen
5 Clear up
6 Psalter
7 Tasmanian
8 Leave footprints
15 Enigmatic
16 Own
18 Ova
20 Estonia
21 Turning
22 Bestial
23 Radiant
27 Chime

66

Across
1 Bailey
4 Affected
9 Licked
10 Minority
12 Reed
13 Sound
14 Toil
17 Disconsolate
20 Bowling-green
23 Exam
24 Raise
25 Manx
28 Pedantic
29 League
30 Touching
31 Amidst

Down
1 Belgrade
2 Increase
3 Eyes
5 Friendliness
6 Ebor
7 Tailor
8 Dry-fly
11 Consultation
15 Rotor
16 Stage
18 Deranged
19 Inexpert
21 Teapot
22 Landau
26 Inch
27 Team

67

Across
 1 Off balance
 6 Afar
 9 Cheapskate
 10 News
 12 Inched
 13 Colander
 15 Time and again
 18 Down the drain
 21 Pastoral
 22 Derive
 24 Isis
 25 Bill-poster
 26 Nigh
 27 Department

Down
 1 Orchid
 2 Fierce
 3 Appreciation
 4 Ankh
 5 Cut corners
 7 Field day
 8 Restring
 11 Paradise Lost
 14 Seven-a-side
 16 Adoption
 17 Twisting
 19 Tiptoe
 20 Ferret
 23 Plea

68

Across
 1 Digger
 4 Polka dot
 8 Sent up
 9 Eminence
 10 Overlies
 11 Onager
 12 Aflutter
 13 Taille
 15 Pander
 18 Shallots
 20 Advent
 21 Exacting
 23 Solecism
 24 Draper
 25 Dear dear
 26 Needed

Down
 1 Disco
 2 Get around
 3 Repaint
 4 Pleasure steamer
 5 Laid out
 6 Donegal
 7 The creeps
 12 Appraised
 14 Ill at ease
 16 Novella
 17 Ratline
 19 Abaddon
 22 Gored

69

Across
 1 Ingratitude
 10 Lid
 11 Impaction
 12 Carnation
 13 Doric
 14 Gosh
 15 Studious
 17 Composes
 19 Maps
 22 Hurst
 23 Lionesses
 25 Imperfect
 26 Oaf
 27 Apologising

Down
 2 Nadir
 3 Repeats
 4 Trivia
 5 Topknots
 6 Decided
 7 Electric chair
 8 Vitriols
 9 Knock spots off
 14 Gumdrops
 16 Well well
 18 Outcrop
 20 Ageless
 21 Sontag
 24 Spoon

70

Across
1 Lissome
5 Hacksaw
9 Caprice
10 Minuses
11 From now on
12 Ouija
13 Reeve
15 Ill at ease
17 Appraises
19 Debar
22 Aroma
23 Preparing
25 Outsize
26 Overall
27 Springe
28 Trainer

Down
1 Lucifer
2 Suppose
3 Orion
4 Edelweiss
5 Human
6 Contorted
7 Sestina
8 Wastage
14 Emanation
16 Lashes out
17 At a loss
18 Plotter
20 Britain
21 Regular
23 Piece
24 Arena

71

Across
1 Square meal
6 Rain
10 Forum
11 Neuralgia
12 Tosspot
13 Elopers
14 Premeditated
18 Dictionaries
21 Overman
23 Hoodlum
24 Raconteur
25 Error
26 Mayo
27 Receptacle

Down
1 Safety
2 Unrest
3 Rump parliament
4 Minuteman
5 Acute
7 Aigrette
8 Nearside
9 Man of the moment
15 Dark horse
16 Ideogram
17 Screechy
19 Cleric
20 Emerge
22 Niece

72

Across
1 Take for a ride
9 Seminar
10 Sawdust
11 Apex
12 Purse
13 Ugli
16 Lattice
17 Sceptre
18 Servant
21 Pitcher
23 Mane
24 Frisk
25 Inca
28 Nowhere
29 Average
30 Hydrotherapy

Down
1 Tempest
2 Kind
3 Fortune
4 Resists
5 Rows
6 Drugget
7 Establishment
8 Strike-breaker
14 Titan
15 Keats
19 Runaway
20 Torrent
21 Passage
22 Hungary
26 Rear
27 Mega

73

Across
1 Camelot
5 Disturb
9 Ruing
10 Bystander
11 Sweetheart
12 Gran
14 Bonfire night
18 Press cutting
21 Earl
22 Stationary
25 Disputant
26 Mount
27 Deserve
28 Saddler

Down
1 Cerise
2 Maiden
3 Lighthouse
4 Table
5 Desert rat
6 Shad
7 Under age
8 Baronets
13 Uninformed
15 Fruitcake
16 Splendid
17 Neurosis
19 Manual
20 Oyster
23 Totes
24 Suer

74

Across
1 Broaches
5 Hold-up
8 At last
9 Eggplant
10 Sold a pup
11 Ashore
12 Plankton
13 Hoof it
15 Tender
18 Pot-belly
20 As well
21 Repealed
23 Dominion
24 Orison
25 Owning
26 Romancer

Down
1 Brass
2 Abandoned
3 Hot spot
4 Sleeping partner
5 Hogwash
6 Draw off
7 Patiently
12 Put paid to
14 Operation
16 Newsman
17 Rolling
19 Taproom
22 Diner

75

Across
1 Toilsome
5 Afraid
9 Resident
10 Grille
12 Agreement
13 Sorts
14 Opus
16 Angling
19 Eye-wash
21 Seth
24 Stern
25 Presented
27 Retain
28 Magazine
29 Strife
30 Tenement

Down
1 Turban
2 Insert
3 Sidle
4 Mincers
6 Foresight
7 Allergic
8 Dressage
11 Etna
15 Plaintiff
17 Censures
18 Repeater
20 Hope
21 Seepage
22 Stride
23 Advent
26 Elate

76

Across
1 Sinister
5 Scoots
9 Estimate
10 Portia
12 Ascend
13 Tolerant
15 Shallow
16 Gear
20 Cant
21 Angered
25 Newsreel
26 Visage
28 Ignite
29 Lakeside
30 Gadget
31 Postcard

Down
1 Seesaw
2 Notice
3 Samantha
4 Efts
6 Closet
7 Outdated
8 Shatters
11 Coroner
14 Blanket
17 Scenting
18 Entwined
19 Sediment
22 Writhe
23 Patina
24 Defend
27 Dado

77

Across
1 Left on the shelf
9 Sangria
10 Attaché
11 Apse
12 Repugnance
14 Thieve
15 Atomiser
17 Beginner
18 Isomer
21 Accountant
22 Snug
24 Trolley
25 Brittle
26 Play gooseberry

Down
1 Last act
2 Finishing school
3 Ours
4 Tracer
5 Evaluate
6 Hit-and-miss
7 Loch Ness monster
8 Meteor
13 Eventually
16 Sentry-go
17 Beauty
19 Roguery
20 Anubis
23 Limb

78

Across
1 Dole
3 Contestant
8 Casino
9 Try again
10 Iritis
11 Imitator
12 Love-hate
14 Rose
16 Oslo
18 Prettier
19 Culverin
20 Meagre
21 Narcissi
22 Neighs
23 Natural gas
24 Tops

Down
1 Deceiver
2 Epistyle
3 Cross over
4 Notwithstanding
5 Startle
6 Acanthus
7 Tenor
13 Trimmings
15 Solleret
16 Organist
17 Obsesses
18 Premier
19 Canon

79

Across
1 Handicap
6 Recite
9 Brazen
10 Alphabet
11 Stand out
12 Notice
13 The bee's knees
16 Single-handed
19 Belted
21 Situated
23 Demotion
24 Adroit
25 As well
26 Lukewarm

Down
2 Aerate
3 Dozen
4 Cantonese
5 Prattle
6 Ripon
7 Chastened
8 Trencher
13 Tightrope
14 Sidetrack
15 Likeness
17 Arsenal
18 Senior
20 Drill
22 Arrow

80

Across
1 Priority
5 Gaelic
9 Champion
10 Prison
11 Footnote
12 Adhere
14 Stuttering
18 Get the sack
22 Report
23 As it were
24 Gloria
25 Pilaster
26 Renege
27 Plangent

Down
1 Pacify
2 In a row
3 Repent
4 Took to task
6 Abridged
7 Listen in
8 Converge
13 Stock-still
15 Agar-agar
16 Step down
17 Charming
19 Strain
20 Settle
21 Regret

www.ingramcontent.com/pod-product-compliance
Ingram Content Group UK Ltd.
Pitfield, Milton Keynes, MK11 3LW, UK
UKHW040640280225
455688UK00002B/33